BOSTON'S
French Secrets

Boston's
French Secrets

Guided Walks That
Reveal Boston's
French Heritage

RHEA HOLLIS ATWOOD

PHOTOGRAPHS BY RAFAEL MILLÁN

Rhea Hollis Atwood

October 9, 2004

Images from the Past
Bennington, Vermont

Author photograph: Mark Millman

Pages 28, 36, and 69: Reproduced from the Dictionary of American Portraits (1967), Dover Publications, Inc.

Page 82: Courtesy Bowdoin College Museum of Art. Reproduced from the Dictionary of American Portraits (1967), Dover Publications, Inc.

Page 127: Courtesy Museum of Fine Arts, Boston

Page 131: Courtesy Paul Revere Memorial Association, Boston

Front and back covers and all other interior photographs: Photographer, Rafael Millán, Watertown, MA

1 2 3 4 5 6 7 8 9 10 XXX 10 09 08 07 06 05 04

First edition

Library of Congress Cataloging-in-Publication Data

Atwood, Rhea Hollis, 1934-
    Boston's French secrets : guided walks that reveal Boston's French heritage / Rhea Hollis Atwood.—1st ed.
    p. cm.
    Includes bibliographical references (p.   ).
    ISBN 1–884592–41–4
    1. French Americans—Massachusetts—Boston—History.
2. French—Massachusetts—Boston—History.   3. Boston
(Mass.)—Tours.   4. Historic sites—Massachusetts—Boston—
Guidebooks.   5. Walking—Massachusetts—Boston—
Guidebooks.   6. Architecture, French—Massachusetts—Boston—
Guidebooks.   7. Arts, French—Massachusetts—Boston—
Guidebooks.   I. Title.
F73.9.F8A88   2004
974.4'6100441—dc22   2004011523

Published by Images from the Past, Inc.
P.O. Box 137, Bennington Vermont 05201
www.imagesfromthepast.com
888-442-3204
Tordis Ilg Isselhardt, Publisher

Printed in the United States
Design and Production: Desktop Miracles, Stowe, VT
Printer: Thomson-Shore, Inc. Dexter, MI

To Paramahansa Yogananda
and
Becca, Ann, and Douglas
and their families

Contents

Acknowledgments

My thanks go to Elaine Uzan Leary, Jane Stahl, and Parivashe Niamir, French Library and Cultural Center/ Alliance Française of Boston and Cambridge; Sally Pierce and Stephen Nonack, Boston Athenaeum; Caron Le Brun, Ritz-Carlton Hotels; Professor Jeff Flagg, Boston College; Eric Jausseran, French Consulate of Boston; Claire Quintal, founding director emerita of the *Institut français* of Assumption College; Cynthia W. Alcorn, Samuel Crocker Lawrence Library, Grand Lodge of Masons in Massachusetts; William and Nellie Dunham, Massachusetts LaFayette Society, Boston; Amelia Carignan and Kena Frank, Boston Museum of Fine Arts; Mario Pereira, Isabella Stewart Gardner Museum; Patrick M. Leehey, Paul Revere House; Boston Center for Adult Education; Reference Department, Boston Public Library; Huguenot Society of America, New York; Father Champagne, The Marist House, Framingham; Paris Musée de la Marine and Paris Centre du Protestantisme; and Alain Tilliette, City Hall Library, Paris.

I would also like to thank coaches and teachers Floyd Kemske, Michael Levin, and Marica Yudkin; supportive friends Pat Clemens, Daniel Jouve, Sonia Landes, Janet and Maurice Ghaly, Beth and Doug Glener, Susan Miller, and Deborrah Henry.

Editor Sarah Novak's thorough attention to detail and ability to suggest a different wording here and there have been invaluable. Ann Gallager, my daughter, has produced a most inspiring and pleasing cover design and for that I give her my special thanks. The photography of Rafael Millán is outstanding and has captured some of the *joie de vivre* for which the French are famous.

Many thanks also go to the Comte Gilbert de Pusy La Fayette for encouraging me to write this book and for his foreword. Thanks are also due Daniel Jouve of Paris for his willingness to introduce the book in France.

The design team of Barry T. Kerrigan and Del LeMond have produced a book with impeccable attention to detail and quality design. An infectious positive attitude and magical computer skills were provided by friend Mark Millman who was always available. Jill Hays acted as the book's picture researcher and her persistence is very appreciated as is the dedicated editing of Peggy Burns. Katrina Martin's research work for the maps has been very helpful.

I would like to thank those who contributed quotes for the book: Jeff Flagg, Comte Gilbert de Pusy La Fayette, Daniel Jouve, Sonia Landes, Claire Quintal, and Consul Général Thierry Vankerk-Hoven.

I wish also to acknowledge the support given to me by the Self-Realization Fellowship communities in Encinitas, California, and Boston, Massachusetts.

And last, a special thanks goes to publisher Tordis Ilg Isselhardt of Images from the Past for her dedication to excellence and her spirited, never-failing guidance. Her encouragement and support have been invaluable.

Foreword

COMTE GILBERT DE PUSY LA FAYETTE

Boston holds a very special place in my heart. Through my association as Honorary Chair of the Massachusetts LaFayette Society, I have made many friends over the years in Boston, New England, and throughout America. In 1990, I attended a ball in Boston to honor the 200th Anniversary of the French Revolution. Since that special occasion I have tried to return every other year to Boston for Massachusetts LaFayette Day on May 20, the anniversary of the death of my ancestor, Marquis de LaFayette, who preferred to be called General LaFayette rather than by any noble trappings. My late mother, whose family was Rochambeau, also joined me on trips to America. She was very active with the DAR, Daughters of the American Revolution. I've enjoyed retracing the steps of many of the sites in Boston General LaFayette visited.

General LaFayette always felt at home whenever he was in Boston. During his farewell tour of America in 1824–25 he made two visits to Boston, with large crowds greeting him in Doric Hall in the State Capitol, Faneuil Hall, and along the streets of Boston. He attended the laying of the foundation of Bunker Hill along with America's great orator and statesman, Senator Daniel Webster.

The Boston area was where the American Revolution began. Both General LaFayette, who was like a son to George Washington, and his son

George Washington LaFayette, received honorary degrees from Harvard. The spirit of the Declaration of Independence came from many of the citizens of Boston and New England. General LaFayette rejoiced in individual freedom and rights. Not known by many, General LaFayette was an early proponent of freedom for all slaves!

The people of Boston left a lasting impression on General LaFayette. One of his best friends lived outside of Boston in Bolton, Massachusetts, Sampson Vryling Stoddard Wilder. In 1824 he visited his old friend in Bolton with the streets lined with lanterns and the local artillery unit renaming themselves the LaFayette Artillery. They spent the night camping outside the Wilder Mansion as LaFayette slept! Throughout his life, LaFayette continued correspondence with many of his Boston friends as well as hosting the visits by many to France.

In addition, I am honored that the Boston area has the International Bilingual School, École Bilingue, come to the State House each May 20 to sing the national anthems of France and America.

I hope in my lifetime to make many more visits to Boston and America. My wife, Iriasema, and I will also make sure our children Alexandre and Caroline will make Boston a second home as it has been for us. In closing, I highly recommend *Boston's French Secrets* for its insights into the history of the French in Boston.

COMTE DE PUSY LA FAYETTE
APRIL 2003

How to Use This Book

Since the French heritage of Boston is not widely known, you are going to be on an archaeological investigation of Boston's French past, a heritage in some cases buried for several hundred years. The focus of these walks is not famous monuments, but rather is a step-by-step exploration of neighborhoods known for their French inhabitants or French architecture. The walker and armchair traveler alike will see Boston's French past up close.

Each walk begins with an easy-to-read map showing the location of the sites of interest in the following tour. The map also gives the nearest subway stations to the walk area. (Maps of Boston's subway system, the oldest in the country, are available at hotels or tourist information centers.)

If possible, read about the tour at home, in your hotel, at a café, or on a park bench, before you begin your walk. Read the Introduction first since the information will explain the flow of French émigrés and visitors to Boston, describing why various groups left France, what they found in Boston, why they are largely unknown, and what they contributed to the city. The "Setting the Stage" section before each walk gives a brief overview of the area covered by the walk. The walk itself contains descriptions of the sites of interest on the tour.

It isn't necessary for you to follow the numbers on the map in order; you can start at any point on the walk.

Cover the walk at your own pace—the tours don't have a time limit. You are free to spend an hour at a museum or library without feeling that you must rush to finish the tour on a schedule. You can even save part of a tour for the next day. These walks are meant to be relaxing and enjoyable, not challenges or marathons.

Be sure to bring your imagination with you. Some of the buildings on the walks are no longer standing and you will need to visualize the mansion or church of the past under its modern exterior. Look for architectural details on buildings not mentioned on the walk, too. If you see a street which looks interesting and it's not on the walk, go ahead and explore it. Don't be afraid to talk to people and ask questions. They may not know about Boston's French connections, but they can help you find your way.

If you want to feel more French yourself, you'll find several opportunities right in Boston. Sit at a sidewalk café and order a café au lait or a mineral water. A list of French restaurants is given at the end of the book—enjoy a dinner or lunch or have a snack at a café or an Au Bon Pain. The French Library and Cultural Center on Walk Five shows French movies, usually with English subtitles, on weekends. If you know some French, you may want to look at a French newspaper or magazine at the library.

The brief chronology at the end of the book will help you to situate yourself in time for important historical events in America and France. For those wishing to know more about Boston's French past, the brief bibliography also found here is a helpful source.

Irish and Irish-American readers may find a surprise in the "So You Think You're Irish" section: the Norman-French invasion of England introduced French names to England and Ireland which appear to be Irish, but are actually French. Also, if you are interested in tracing your family background, sources for genealogical research are listed. If you think you have French ancestors, these genealogy sources will help you find your French heritage.

Enjoy exploring the city's French connections. Block by block you will see more of Boston's French culture, past and present. Soon you will feel surrounded by things French, and Boston's streets will be filled with new meaning and a new appreciation for the men and women who have contributed to the city's rich culture.

Introduction

French heritage in Boston? Hardly! It's more an English or Irish city, you would say. So did I until I chanced to discover a tablet on Franklin Street. It commemorated the residence of the Reverend Jean Louis Lefebvre de Cheverus, a French priest who arrived in 1796 and who became Boston's first Catholic bishop. I hadn't realized that French people had immigrated to Boston and wanted to know more. Besides, ten years earlier I had lived in Paris for two years and was hungry for more French contact.

During the following years I did more research and tracked down more clues. I found that no book had been written about all the different French groups which had come to Boston. Eventually I started giving walking tours of Boston's French heritage at the Boston Center for Adult Education, and for the French Library and Cultural Center/Alliance Française of Boston and Cambridge, and other Boston institutions. Students suggested that I write a book and this is the result, the first book written about Boston's French, past and present. I found an exciting group of men and women who have enriched Boston's culture and history in magnificent ways and against many odds which I wish to share with you, the reader, especially since many of them for the most part were unknown and undiscovered. I wanted to know why they came here and why their French background was not mentioned in Boston's history books.

French men and women seldom find a sufficient reason to leave their country, so what compelled them to immigrate to Boston? The following is what I found. Let's begin with the first arrivals.

The Frenchmen Samuel de Champlain and Sieur de Monts sailed into Massachusetts Bay in 1605, far ahead of the English, and landed on Noddle's Island in the harbor, calling it *La Nouvelle France*, or "New France." Their efforts at colonization, however, were focused farther north and in 1630 the English triumphantly claimed Boston for the crown. The British brought with them a strong dislike for the French, which set the stage for future generations.

The first group from France to arrive in large numbers was the fleeing Huguenots, or French Protestants, who were influenced by the religious teachings of John Calvin. They were escaping persecution, even murder, by French Roman Catholics during the French Wars of Religion, which began in 1562. The Catholic Church sought to eradicate all minority religions, or *sects*, in France by conversion—or death. *Dragonnades,* or raids, were held across France, particularly in the Protestant stronghold of southwestern France. The raiders entered homes at night, murdering the adult occupants and taking the children to be reared in Catholic homes. During the St. Bartholomew's Day massacre of 1572, thousands of Huguenots were slaughtered in Paris and the provinces. According to nineteenth-century historian Leopold von Ranke, the massacre of men, women, and children killed twice as many in a few days than were killed over three years during the French Revolution. Figures cited in different accounts vary widely, but go as high as ten thousand in Paris and twenty to fifty thousand across France.

During a temporary peace in the Wars of Religion, Henry IV of Navarre, himself a Protestant, married Marguerite de Valois, sister of King Charles IX of France. When Henry converted to Catholicism, he famously said, "Paris was worth a mass." To soften this compromise, Henry issued the Edict of Nantes in 1598, which restored some civil and religious rights to the Huguenots, including public worship, public assembly, and marriage. However, despite the edict, Huguenots began to leave France to seek safety in surrounding countries and later in Boston in the New World. Those who left early were able to liquidate their holdings and take money with them. In 1685, Louis XIV revoked the Edict of Nantes, removing from the Protestants their hard-earned liberties.

The persecution and killing increased. Many Huguenots converted to Catholicism and stayed in France, but others hastily fled their country, possibly as many as four hundred thousand, leaving behind families, homes, businesses, money, and land. They sought refuge in England, Ireland, the German Palatinate, Switzerland, and North America, and even as far away as southern Africa and South America. It was a diaspora of great proportions. These émigrés were a highly skilled population: merchants, doctors, blacksmiths, gunsmiths, distillers, financiers, goldsmiths, clock smiths, textile workers, artists, and jewelry makers.

Starting at the end of the seventeenth century and into the eighteenth, several hundred Huguenots came to Boston, the Protestant center of the New World.

(Since names were often changed, as well as occupation and religion, exact numbers are hard to cite.) The New World was also regarded as a utopia, a paradise free from the ills of the Old World, by influential eighteenth-century French writers, such as Voltaire.

Distance from Catholic officials was also appealing. The fear of Catholic reprisal and a need to enter the Boston business world helped inspire the Huguenots' urge to assimilate as quickly as possible into Boston culture. As a result, in one or two generations there was little or no trace of their French heritage. Thus, this aspect of Boston's French culture remains largely unknown.

Many changed their names: *Rivoire* became Revere, *Baudouin* became Bowdoin. They married wealthy English wives of good social standing, and changed their occupation and their religion—in short, were willing to give up their heritage in order to survive. These strong, talented, and courageous people helped build Boston; their contributions are noted in the walks to follow.

The Acadians were the next group of French to arrive in Boston. These simple, rural, peaceful people were farmers and fishermen who came to Nova Scotia and the adjoining Maritime provinces from France in 1604. The name *Acadia* is said to be from the French for Arcadia, a legendary region of pastoral peace and simplicity. The colony passed back and forth between British and French hands in the years to come. The Acadians chose neutrality, fearing that if they signed an oath with the British they would be forced to fight their fellow Frenchmen if England went to war with France.

When 1755 came and war seemed imminent, British authorities in Nova Scotia decided to deport the neutral Acadians to the American colonies, fearing they would side with the French against the British. And so it was that in 1755 two thousand Acadians were sent into exile, surrendering their homes and land, and taking with them only their household goods, if that. Many families were separated. Of the two thousand, 735 were sent to Massachusetts.

As a result of overcrowding, exposure to the cold, disease, and malnutrition, many died on the journey. In Boston, unprepared for such an influx, immediate care for the survivors was hastily improvised. The Acadians had little knowledge of earning a living in a city, and so, much of the burden for their welfare fell to the city of Boston and anonymous givers, particularly the Quakers. Dr. Nathan Tufts was noted for his generous treatment of the sick. A few years after the Treaty of Paris in 1763, most of the Acadians returned to Nova Scotia, although some went to France.

The Acadians left little visible trace of their time in Boston, but their strong religious faith and close family ties were an example for all to follow. Magistrates record that they were "never drunk, never disorderly, and never before a magistrate." Governor Gage of Massachusetts said that the Acadians were "remarkable for the simplicity of their manners, the order of their piety and the purity of their morals." Longfellow's poem "Evangeline," about an Acadian woman separated from her beloved, captured many hearts. Though little in evidence, the story of the Acadian eleven-year exile in Boston has not been forgotten.

War was again the reason for the next group of Frenchmen, who arrived in Boston to help the colonies in their fight for freedom from Britain, with French military expertise and money for munitions. A royal fleet of warships from France arrived in Boston in 1778 under the command of Admiral Count d'Estaing; his officers and sailors soon overcame the prejudices of even well-educated Bostonians toward the French. Bostonians took pride in the dedication of d'Estaing and army generals Lafayette and Rochambeau to the American cause, and came to regard their allies with gratitude and affection. When the Boston campaign was over and the fleet left, several families and single men stayed behind in Boston to start a new life in the New World, adding to the growing French connection.

The next arrivals in Boston from France, like the Huguenots before them, were also fleeing for their lives, French priests who refused to support the harsh Civil Constitution of the Clergy instituted during the French Revolution. Father Lefebvre de Cheverus, a notable member of this group, brought much devotion and scholarship to his post in Boston, arriving in 1796. Many other priests followed, contributing to the growing Roman Catholic Church in Boston. Boston's first Catholic bishop, de Cheverus was beloved by Boston Catholics and Protestants alike. Hundreds of petitions from both Catholics and Protestants sought to retain him when he was recalled to France near the end of his career.

French architecture arrived in Boston in the nineteenth century with architects returning to Boston from their studies in Paris, enthusiastic about new French styles. French Academic, Second Empire, and Beaux Arts buildings began to appear in the city, as well as the new Parisian style of urban planning. The 1920s and 1930s saw Art Deco and Art Nouveau buildings copied from Paris begin to line the streets of Boston's financial district and downtown Boston.

A Francophone, or French-speaking, group sought relief in Boston in the mid-1800s and early 1900s not because of religious persecution, but from great economic need. These were French Canadians from Canada, where their small farms on poor land, combined with a short growing season, were not very productive. Seasonal lumbering in the winter brought in only a little additional cash. The large families of ten or twelve children which the Catholic Church advocated were difficult to feed in these circumstances.

The problems of subsistence farming coincided with heightened economic activity across the border in New England, a result of the Industrial Revolution and the new mill towns on rivers supplying inexpensive electric power for the manufacture of textiles and leather goods. No skills were needed for these factory jobs; even children could be put to work in the mills, enabling a family of twelve to earn up to $40 a week. When the first French Canadians returned to visit in Canada they were well dressed with money to spend, which did not go unnoticed by their former neighbors. By 1850 some twenty thousand French Canadians had immigrated during the five years before, although record-keeping at the Canadian border was scanty.

Most of the French Canadians headed for the mill towns surrounding Boston; discouraged by the higher rents and cost of living, and a lack of skills for urban work, only a few of them came to live in the city. Those who came in subsequent generations were largely in the professional class or were artists and musicians. Since there weren't many French Canadians in Boston, there was no French section of the city. Several French families, however, were attracted to the vicinity of Our Lady of Victories Church on Isabella Street, "the French Church," which held masses in French for years. Some small shops were set up in Boston for the making of hand-crafted articles. Boston served largely as a central meeting place for the many French-Canadian groups around New England formed to promote their culture and community.

These groups include La Société Historique Franco-Américaine, established in 1899 as a forum for French-Canadian cultural needs. The society's members were of the professional class, meeting at the Harvard Club or at a Boston restaurant. This group is still active. The Comité de Vie Franco-Américaine was an umbrella organization formed to encourage the growth of local groups throughout New England; its aims were both cultural and social and a convention was held every two years. La Fédération Féminine Franco-Américaine met from 1951 until 2001 when it disbanded.

In 1881, the Massachusetts State House in Boston was the scene of a protest against negative treatment of French Canadians by the chief of the Department of Labor, Colonel Wright. The French Canadians proved their case that their strong religious faith, willingness to work, and close-knit families were valuable assets and had a positive influence on Bostonians and on New Englanders in general.

The most recent Francophone immigrants to Boston are from French-speaking countries such as Haiti, Guadeloupe, Martinique, Switzerland, Belgium, Morocco, Lebanon, Senegal, and French Cameroon. French- and French Creole–speaking Haitians constitute one of the largest groups to immigrate to Boston, coming here in large numbers in the early 1970s for a combination of political and economic reasons, including the oppressiveness of the Duvalier dictatorship and lack of work. The 2000 Federal Census lists forty-four thousand Haitians living in Boston, the majority settling in the Mattapan and Dorchester sections of the city.

The many unique cultures of these Francophone peoples have added immeasurably to Boston's culture and continue to create a Boston of diversity and sophistication.

As you travel block by block through Boston, the French influence here, past and present, will come alive. You will appreciate more deeply the French and Francophone contributions to Boston in statesmanship, art, architecture, city planning, music, cuisine, fashion, education, and many other areas. The drama of French hardships and daring becomes more evident, too, as the story of how many sacrificed their heritage for a chance to live and worship in freedom is revealed.

Boston's French Secrets does not claim to be an exhaustive source of things French, but wishes to stimulate readers and researchers to make their own investigations. You'll no doubt find your own French secrets as you go along and participate in some of that French *joie de vivre*, or joy of living. I hope that French and Francophone residents and visitors will also find this guide an inspiration for tracing their heritage in Boston. It's time that Boston claims its French legacy and enjoys all its gifts.

Rhea Hollis Atwood
Encinitas, California
March 2004

The Walks

Old City Hall

Downtown Boston

A Huguenot Merchant Prince,
Tributes to General Lafayette,
and French Distilleries

❧ SETTING THE STAGE ❧

The legacy of the Huguenots in Boston is sometimes evident and sometimes requires a little imaginative reconstruction. This walk leads to the sites of their church, their homes, their businesses, and their final resting places, and considers how the austere Puritans reacted to these warm, friendly, and sometimes flamboyant newcomers.

Memorabilia of Paul Revere, a second-generation Huguenot, and of General Lafayette, both important figures in the American Revolution, are also found on this walk.

The importance of various French architectural styles in Boston—and from here throughout the United States—is also apparent on these downtown streets.

Although several of the buildings relating to French interest are missing because of fire, so-called

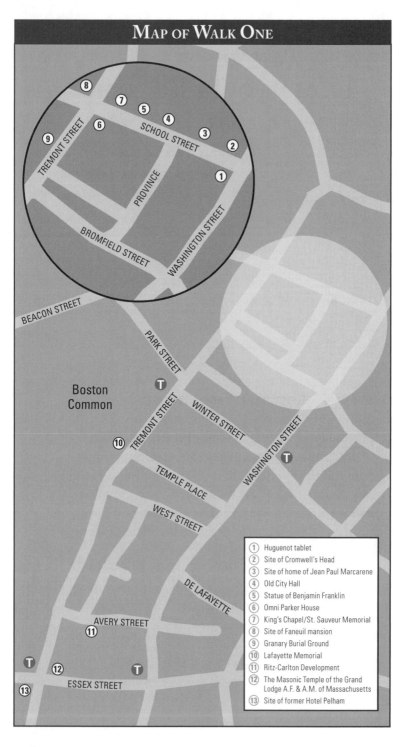

MAP OF WALK ONE

BEACON STREET

TREMONT STREET

SCHOOL STREET

PROVINCE

WASHINGTON STREET

BROMFIELD STREET

PARK STREET

Boston
Common

TREMONT STREET

WINTER STREET

WASHINGTON STREET

TEMPLE PLACE

WEST STREET

DE LAFAYETTE

AVERY STREET

ESSEX STREET

① Huguenot tablet
② Site of Cromwell's Head
③ Site of home of Jean Paul Marcarene
④ Old City Hall
⑤ Statue of Benjamin Franklin
⑥ Omni Parker House
⑦ King's Chapel/St. Sauveur Memorial
⑧ Site of Faneuil mansion
⑨ Granary Burial Ground
⑩ Lafayette Memorial
⑪ Ritz-Carlton Development
⑫ The Masonic Temple of the Grand
   Lodge A.F. & A.M. of Massachusetts
⑬ Site of former Hotel Pelham

urban progress, and neglect, the layout of School and Tremont streets in particular has been altered very little over the past three hundred years. Thus, the walker will have the satisfaction of being on ground relatively undisturbed by change—all too rare in America's fast-moving cities.

──────────── ⟨ **THE WALK** ⟩ ────────────

A tablet in the first recessed doorway at **24 School Street** commemorates the site of the temple of the **Huguenots,** or French Protestants, in Boston. The plaque reads as follows:

①

ON THIS SITE STOOD

THE CHURCH OF THE

FRENCH HUGUENOTS 1716–1741

USED AS A CONGREGATIONAL

CHURCH 1748–1788

OCCUPIED BY

ROMAN CATHOLICS 1788–1803

FIRST PUBLIC MASS

CELEBRATED IN BOSTON

NOVEMBER 2 – 1788

THIS TABLET PLACED BY THE CITY OF BOSTON

1925

Facing murder, religious persecution, and denial of civil rights by Catholics in France during the country's religious wars, these Huguenots fled from France in the late 1600s and early 1700s seeking religious freedom and their rights as citizens. (More about the story of the Huguenots is in the Introduction.)

Many Huguenots converted to Catholicism, but others sought asylum in England, the Netherlands, Ireland, Germanic regions, and many other countries. Several hundred sought safety in Boston, then the center of the Protestant religion in the New World. Life in this new paradise would leave the ills of the Old World behind. The exact number of these French Protestant émigrés to Boston is unknown, since records are inaccurate: many changed their names as well as religion and country of origin to avoid detection and possible reprisal.

The Boston Huguenots met every Sunday at a building that had been part of Boston Public Latin School, now covered over by the east end of King's Chapel and parts of the Old City Hall. They worshiped here for thirty years since their request for a bigger place was consistently and harshly refused by town officials, who said that the spot had been good enough for them "for some time past and it would accommodate them for some time to come." Finally, the officials relented, and the Huguenots raised $1,300 to erect a small brick church near the present plaque. Some of the church (or temple) members included the families of Boutineau, Bowdoin, Brimmer, Chardon, Dumaresque, Dupee, Faneuil, Johonnot, Mascarene, Revere, and Sigourney.

The town officials were still unhappy with the Huguenots. Their church services were not in English, for example. Then, some married Huguenot couples were seen kissing each other after services on the church steps, outraging Puritan sensibilities. Furthermore, Boston judge Samuel Sewall (known as the "hanging judge" because he presided over the Salem witch trials) criticized Huguenot pastor Pierre Daille vehemently in public "about his partaking with the French Church on the 25th of December on account on its being Christ-mas, as they abusively call it." The Puritans made no observance of this day and would have regarded the Huguenots' singing and feasting as works of the Devil. A law was passed in Boston in 1651 stating that "whosoever shall be found observing any such day as Christmas, or the like, either by forbearing labor, feasting, or any other way upon such account as aforesaid, every such person so offendingly, shall apply for every such offense, five shillings as a fine of the country."

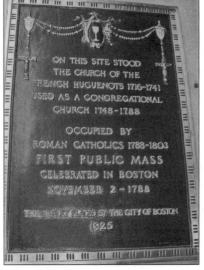

Huguenot tablet, 24 School Street

Complain as they may, the townspeople of Boston benefited from the French warmth of family bonds and joyful observance of religious celebrations. The stern Puritan rigidity of Boston at the time was tempered by their presence. Writers Allan Forbes and Paul Cadman noted that the sunniness of Paul Revere, a second-generation Huguenot, and his oak-like strength, "are the gifts that Paul Revere inherited from his French father, the exile who was one of those great Huguenots who infused cheerfulness into our stolid Puritan ways." In the poet Rudyard Kipling's words the Huguenots were "the light sane joy of life, the buckler of the Gaul."

In fact, Puritan sentiment was not all against the Huguenots. Puritan minister Cotton Mather referred to the Huguenots as the "Saints in France" and indicated that if they suffered that meant trouble for Protestants everywhere, including the Puritans. In 1682, when the first Huguenots arrived, the Massachusetts Council welcomed them warmly, took up a collection for the financially distressed immigrants, who had left much behind, and called for a day of fasting and prayer on their behalf.

The church was closed in 1748 when the parishioners had dwindled in number. However, this was not a sign of failure, but of success, as the Huguenots had rapidly assimilated into Boston society at various levels. Even though the Huguenots had stipulated that the church always be used by Protestant groups, in 1788 one of Boston's first Catholic churches began holding services in the building; the first public Roman Catholic mass in Boston was celebrated here on November 2 of that year.

Before leaving this spot, note that a French minister of this Huguenot church was responsible for the first publication in French in the North American British colonies, in 1690—his attack on the Jesuit-Indian Catholic catechism (though it was printed in Canada). This pleased some of Boston's old Puritan elite and Huguenots alike.

An active stagecoach inn and tavern called **Cromwell's Head** was located at **19 School Street.** The famous tavern was visited by the French officer and author Marquis François Jean de Chastellux in 1782 before he called on M. de Vaudreuil, an officer of the French fleet during the American Revolution.

The Niles Building at **27 School Street** was where **Jean Paul Marcarene**, a Huguenot, lived in a two-story white brick house. He was a major general in the English army and served as lieutenant governor of Nova Scotia from 1740 to 1749. After his death and the end of the Revolution, his family went back to Canada, since they were royalists.

Across the street from the Huguenot tablet is the **Boston Jewels** shop at **23 School Street**, specializing in watches from France and the French area of Switzerland. This is noteworthy since many of the original Huguenots were jewelers, or workers in fine metals. The owner, Mori Mosavi, lived in France for ten years and speaks French, further adding to this "noncoincidence."

At **45 School Street** is the **Old City Hall**, an elaborate fantasy piece of Second Empire architecture, which strongly resembles the Jesuit church Saint-Paul-Saint-Louis in the Marais district of Paris. Designed by Boston architects Gridley J. Fox Bryant and Arthur Gilman, it was built in 1862–1865. ④

The Second Empire style was popular during the reign of Napoleon III (1852–1871), the next empire after that of Napoleon I. The building of the "new Louvre," an addition to the original building and one of the first examples of the style in Paris, sparked great interest in this new architecture, which Boston was later to adopt. In the United States, the style became so closely associated with the Grant administration (1869–1877) that it was also called the "General Grant Style."

The style is known for its love of ornamentation and the distinctive mansard roof. Named for seventeenth-century French architect François Mansart, this type of roof has two steep slopes on all four sides, usually accompanied by single or twin dormer windows. Nineteenth-century Boston engineers, puzzled by the name of this innovation, simply wrote "French roof" on their architectural designs and insurance drawings where the word mansard should have been. The first mansard roof west of the Atlantic was created in 1848 in Boston by the Parisian architect Charles Lemoulnier for the Deacon mansion, no longer standing, but originally on Washington Street near the outskirts of the

city. (Some pieces from the mansion are on display at Boston's Museum of Fine Arts in its new gallery of eighteenth-century French decorative arts).

Old City Hall has a large central pavilion, which goes high above the mansard roof, a large base, and two levels with arched windows topped by dormers. Affectionately called "the white wedding cake," Old City Hall is one of the country's first examples of historic preservation and adaptive reuse. Slated for demolition when the new City Hall was built, the building was rescued and renovated for modern offices

Statue of Benjamin Franklin

and a restaurant in 1969–1970 by Anderson and Notter Associates. The building is now home to several office suites and, until recently, Maison Robert, for thirty-three years a classic French restaurant.

The statues in the green space in front of Old City Hall continue the French theme. The statue of **Benjamin Franklin** on the left, in 1856 Boston's first portrait statue, celebrates the drafter of the alliance between Louis XVI and the new American republic. **Josiah Quincy** on the right was a mayor of Boston. He was also the good friend of **Count Nicholas Marie Alexandre Vattemare**, French visionary and public

⑤

library enthusiast. Vattemare once sent Boston a gift of fifty practical French books, but they languished, unused, in their crate in Old City Hall for several years. For the complete story, see the description of the Boston Public Library in Walk Five.

As you near the head of School Street stop to look at a plaque on the sidewalk in front of the Old City Hall commemorating the **Boston Public Latin School**. Founded in 1635, it has the honor of being the oldest public school in America with a continuous existence. Famous graduates of Boston Latin include Samuel Adams, John Hancock, Benjamin Franklin, Charles Bulfinch, and Huguenot descendant James Bowdoin II. Bowdoin was sent to the esteemed Latin School as part of the Huguenot assimilation process. Here and at Harvard, the next step for his education and social standing, he could become acquainted with the sons of Boston's first families. You will learn more about the remarkable Bowdoin family on Walk Four.

The **Omni Parker House** at **60 School Street**, which ⑥ claims to be the longest continuously operating hotel in America, had its beginnings on the site of a property purchased by Huguenot Joseph Mico (Micault). The land he purchased equals approximately the size of the present Omni Parker House. In 1707 Micault built a grand brick mansion here for his wife, the wealthy Miss Brattle of Brattle Street, Cambridge.

In 1833 Harvey Parker, a Maine farm boy, established an inn on Court Street called "Parker's." The

farmer-turned-innkeeper was known for his insistence on excellent food, so few were surprised when in 1855 he paid his imported French chef, Sanzian, the lavish salary of $5,000 per year. It was this year that Parker acquired the School Street site, where he constructed a European-style hotel, which separated charges for room and board, and served meals continuously. It hosted such personages as Charles Dickens, Willa Cather, and France's renowned Sarah Bernhardt. Dubbed the

King's Chapel

"grande dame of hotels," its numerous additions have earned it the title of the "French chateau."

At **58 Tremont Street** stands **King's Chapel**, the first Anglican Church in Boston, founded in 1686 to serve British officers. The Puritans and colonists in general looked on it with disfavor. Originally a wooden structure, the present church building was constructed from 1749 to 1754; dark Quincy granite forms walls four feet thick. The elaborate steeple was never built due to lack of funds. After the evacuation of Boston by the British, only a few Anglican families stayed behind. Under the leadership of James Freeman, King's Chapel became the first Unitarian church in America in 1787. The adjoining graveyard, dating from 1631, is the oldest in the city.

Of interest to Francophiles is a large pyramid-shaped tombstone at the corner of the cemetery to the left of the chapel as you face it. It is the site of the grave of the **Chevalier de St. Sauveur**, first chamberlain to the Comte d'Artois, the younger brother of Louis XVI, and thus a direct link to the royal family of France. St. Sauveur, an officer in the naval forces sent by France in support of the colonies during the Revolution, was killed near King's Chapel on September 15, 1778, in a late-night skirmish between Boston colonists and members of the French navy.

St. Sauveur Memorial

Fearful that the death would escalate into a large-scale riot, the officer's comrades hastily dragged the body in secret down to the lower vaults of King's Chapel. There in a vault that night a private funeral mass was held for St. Sauveur, the first use of the Roman, or Catholic, rite in Boston. A monument in honor of the slain officer was to be erected by Boston authorities. However, the obelisk was neither made nor placed in that spot until 1917, when a sharp-eyed clerk caught the omission. The lapse of 139 years was termed a "bureaucratic error," but it seems more likely to be part of the New England tradition of suspicion towards anything French. The inscription on the stone, in French, tells St. Sauveur's story.

King's Chapel is open for services and guided tours. It is wheelchair accessible, with space for a wheelchair during services and concerts.

Opposite King's Chapel is the lackluster high-rise **One Beacon Street**, which houses the Sovereign Bank on the Tremont Street side. On this site was once the handsome mansion of wealthy **André Faneuil**, a Huguenot merchant. He was able to escape La Rochelle in southwestern France with some money and became one of the most wealthy and respected merchants of Boston. The Faneuils refused to Anglicize their name, unlike many other Huguenots, with the result that the Yankees were able to say only "Funel." It is that name which was originally placed on the family tombstone in the Granary Burial Ground (described below). The Faneuil fortune was to go to the one of his two nephews, Peter

Peter Faneuil

or Benjamin, who did not marry. When Benjamin married, **Peter Faneuil** (1700–1743)—not married but perhaps not without companionship either—inherited the Faneuil wealth and set out to live a life of extravagance and ease.

As you stand on the sidewalk with your back to the King's Chapel fence, imagine an imposing mansion across from you. Pemberton Hill ascended steeply behind it, with seven acres of gardens. The summer pavilion at its summit rose high above the city and afforded a magnificent view of Boston and the surrounding harbor. It had at its peak a gilded grasshopper similar to the one on Faneuil Hall, symbolizing prosperity, some say.

The Faneuil mansion was an early example of Boston's increasing interest in French taste. In the late eighteenth century the Boston of the new republic turned to France for inspiration in creating a cultured and democratic mode of living. Britain was no longer considered the only arbiter of taste and style. Comte Louis-Philippe de Ségur wrote that "Boston affords a proof that democracy and luxury are not incompatible, for in no part of the United States is so much comfort or a more agreeable society to be found." (The French count's judgment of American cities is trustworthy: he fought in the American Revolution, and was a diplomat, historian, poet, and author.)

The Faneuil mansion's hothouse, or glass greenhouse, the first in America, was widely admired. Bostonians began to imitate French design in gardens and landscaping. Merchant Timothy Pickering of Salem sent seeds from Marseille, France, to Boston statesman George Cabot in 1799. Boston's millionaire China merchant, Colonel Handasyd Perkins, who lived for several years in France, imported many exotic plants for his Brookline estate to create gardens in the current French style. The libraries of American architect Charles Bulfinch and his contemporaries were known to have books illustrating French plans for gardens and landscapes, which inspired their designs for the new countryseats they were creating in the Boston area. The First List of Honorary Members of the Massachusetts Horticultural Society of 1829 gives strong proof of the prevalent French influence. It includes such names as M. Herecart de Thury, President of the Horticultural Society of Paris; General de La Fayette at his home, La Grange; and Mons. Philippe André Vilmorin, Paris, whose family still operates a large seed and plant firm in Paris, parts of which can be still be seen today along the right bank of the Seine River.

There is more to know about the mysterious Peter Faneuil. The wealthiest man in Boston in his day, Faneuil proceeded down School Street on his way to church in his brightly polished coach, with liveried staff equally gleaming. Puritan disapproval of things French at the shocking sight of Peter Faneuil's flaunting appearance can be imagined. (Even the executives at One Beacon

Street might register their disapproval.) Faneuil owned fourteen hundred ounces of silver plate, including "a large handsome chamber pot." Some of the pieces are on display at the Boston Museum of Fine Arts. His cellars were bursting at all times with wine, beer, and arrack, a fermented drink made with palm sap and molasses plus quantities of Cheshire and Gloucester cheese.

To widespread surprise, however, Faneuil offered the town governing body a large sum of money to build a new town hall. The offer was refused twice—the delay another example of anti-French sentiment? Finally, the board assented and plans progressed for this generous gift originating in French soil. The hall was designed to have meeting places on the first or upper floor and a market underneath, as in France.

Peter Faneuil died suddenly at the age of forty-two; Faneuil Hall's first public ceremony was his funeral oration, in which there was no mention of his French descent. In 1783 his home was confiscated by the Commonwealth.

Several Boston charities today still carry the name of Faneuil, a reminder of continuing Huguenot generosity.

⑨ The **Granary Burial Ground**, an illustrious cemetery begun in 1660, is the final resting place for 2,300 early Bostonians. It took its name from the granary which stood at the corner of Park Street; the land was let out each year for pasturage for neighboring animals. Three signers of the Declaration of Independence, nine governors, and Boston's first mayor are found here. Several French men and women, and their descendants—the famous and those of less renown who leavened the daily life of Boston—are also interred here. The grave of the great patriot Paul Revere is here, as well as those of members of the Faneuil family and Governor Bowdoin and his family. The Faneuil family

Granary Burial Ground

vault is found at the rear on the left side of the cemetery; the Bowdoin family vault is to its left.

Also in a group in the center are several other Huguenot graves marking the men and women of more modest means. You may want to visit the tombstone of Huguenot Andrew Johonnot's wife, Susannah, which is to the left of the large central Franklin family monument as you face north with your back to Tremont Street. From the front left of the Franklin monument follow the third row down twenty-one gravestones and you will find the highest marker in the line, inscribed with these well-known lines:

> STOP HERE MY FRIENDS AND CAST AN EYE
>
> AS YOU ARE NOW SO ONCE WAS I.
>
> AS I AM NOW SO YOU MUST BE.
>
> PREPARE FOR DEATH AND FOLLOW ME.

On the top of the stone is carved the face of a stern woman with vines reaching down each side of her face. The tombstone is quite tall, standing out among the other more modest size stones in this area of ordinary shopkeepers and artisans. A Frenchman seeing Susannah Johonnot's stone wondered immediately why the verse wasn't in French. The Huguenots' speedy assimilation, as opposed to slow integration, was the answer.

Several other French tombstones seem to cluster here for conviviality or protection. Peace Cazneau, whose tomb is the fourth grave to the left of Susannah Johonnot's, was admitted into the Colony of Massachusetts in 1691 in Boston. He returned to Boston after the ending of the Oxford Colony, a Huguenot settlement near present-day Worcester, where he became a prosperous felt-maker. This idyllic colony complete with a gristmill, vineyards, and church had to be abandoned because of repeated Indian attacks. However, in a history of the early Huguenots in Boston he is listed as Paix Cazneau, the French equivalent of Peace. Could it be that a gravestone carver felt that a foreign name was not fitting for a Puritan cemetery? Or perhaps Cazneau changed his name later in his life.

Opposite the corner of **Tremont and Temple streets** and the **Stearns Building** at **140 Tremont Street** you will find the **Lafayette Memorial**. This modest marker, nestled under the trees of the Boston Common along what is called the "Lafayette Mall," reflects America's gratitude to this great statesman and soldier. Lafayette's triumphal return to Boston in 1824 was along this general route. The monument, about seven feet high, shows Lafayette's fine profile and has the following inscription:

THE LAFAYETTE MALL

THIS MALL WAS NAMED IN HONOR

OF MARQUIS DE LAFAYETTE

DISTINGUISHED FRENCH SOLDIER

MAJOR GENERAL IN THE WAR OF AMERICAN INDEPENDENCE

AND ILLUSTRIOUS PATRIOT OF THE FRENCH REVOLUTION

WHO NOBLY SERVED THE CAUSE

OF LIBERTY ON TWO CONTINENTS

INVITED BY ACT OF CONGRESS TO REVISIT THE UNITED STATES

AS A GUEST OF THE NATION IN 1824

HE WAS WELCOMED WITH SIGNAL HONOR

AS HE PASSED ALONG THIS MALL

HE LAID THE CORNER-STONE OF BUNKER HILL MONUMENT

JUNE 17, 1825

"HEAVEN SAW FIT TO ORDAIN THAT THE ELECTRIC

SPARK OF LIBERTY SHOULD BE CONDUCTED THROUGH

YOU FROM THE NEW WORLD TO THE OLD."

ERECTED BY THE CITY OF BOSTON 1924

Young Lafayette was determined to come to America to aid the colonists in their cause. When his parents refused to help him, Lafayette, then nineteen, bought a ship with his own money, outfitted it, and hired a crew. He was placed under General Washington's command and they soon developed a close relationship as the young Lafayette demonstrated his military skills and loyalty to the colonists. He acted skillfully as a liaison between American and French military leaders, often urging them to put aside petty differences and address themselves to the winning of the war.

Lafayette's attachment to the city of Boston was one of great affection and concern, and his warm feelings were amply returned by Bostonians. He visited Boston three times during the American Revolution to aid the colonists and give them support. He then made a triumphal return in 1824 and 1825 when he was a guest of honor throughout the United States. In

a letter to a Massachusetts senator, he wrote, "In whatever part of the United States I shall find myself, on reaching the shores of America, I shall lose no time in my eagerness to revisit the city of Boston." In a letter to his wife Adrienne about his reception in Boston in 1824, he noted, "There was no love and affection that the crowd did not give me as they escorted me out of the city." Lafayette paid another tribute to the city, according to tradition, when he took dirt from the Bunker Hill monument area to be put on his grave in France. His role in obtaining victory for the colonists in the American Revolution cannot be underestimated nor his place in the hearts of Bostonians.

Lafayette Memorial

Each year on LaFayette Day, held on May 20, members of the LaFayette Society of America place a wreath on the memorial and hold a reception and luncheon in honor of LaFayette. Every few years, the Comte de La Fayette, a direct descendant of the general, visits Boston from his home in Paris with his family to take part in these ceremonies.

Notice the ornate marquee on the building opposite the monument, which was once the staid department store, R.H. Stearns. The balconies and seashell scroll motifs are elements of the French architectural style called Beaux Arts found throughout the city; more examples are pointed out in following walks.

Also along Lafayette's triumphal tour route, off **Tremont Street** at **10 Avery Street** between West and Boylston streets, is the high-density, high-rise, mixed-use **Ritz-Carlton Development**, winner of an award from the Congress for the New Urbanism. Like its Paris and Boston predecessors, this Ritz-Carlton exudes taste and elegance, and its international-style decor is designed to welcome guests from the nearby financial and entertainment districts. The $515 million complex provides a myriad of services: in its two buildings which face each other across Avery Street are 193 Ritz-Carlton hotel rooms, 399 condominium apartments, nineteen movie screens, sixty-three "extended-stay" suites for business guests, and a sports club spacious enough for two football fields, plus several restaurants, shops, and bars; all are handicapped accessible. An underground garage has 1,100 parking spaces.

(11)

General Lafayette

The complex is located near Avenue de Lafayette, and Lafayette Place, named, of course, for America's favorite French icon. After Lafayette's grand tour of America in 1824 and 1825, streets named for him sprung up all over the country. Another irony in its location is the fact that Avery Street was the site of many distilleries run by Huguenots.

This street played a role in the famous "rum triangle" of the 1700s. Enslaved black Africans were brought to the French West Indies and North America to work on sugar cane plantations. Molasses made from the sugar cane was then shipped to Boston where it was distilled to make rum. The rum was sent back to Africa where it bought more workers and continued the triangle. A Huguenot named Daniel Johonnot had distilleries on Avery Street and on Change Street, as did other Huguenots in this business.

(12) **The Masonic Temple of the Grand Lodge A.F. & A.M. of Massachusetts,** farther down on the left at **186 Tremont Street,** holds many items relating to its past and several French-related pieces. The Masons, or Freemasons as they are also called, are an international fraternal organization with its origins in the Middle Ages in Europe in guilds of skilled craftsmen. Many of the leaders of the Revolution were Masons, including Paul Revere, General Lafayette, Benjamin Franklin, and George Washington. The Provincial Grand Lodge of Massachusetts Masons was first organized in

Paul Revere

Massachusetts in April of 1733 and often met in taverns, which then served as clubs and political forums as well as places to drink and eat. The present building was built in 1899 and, although its interior is austere, the Revere and Lafayette memorabilia are worth the visit.

Paul Revere was a second-generation Huguenot, a fact that has not been widely known until recently. His father, Apollos Rivoire, left the sunny Midi section of France in 1715 when he was thirteen to escape the Huguenot massacres. He was apprenticed to a worker in fine metals in Boston, a common Huguenot occupation. He also followed a general pattern for Huguenots by changing his last name.

After considering such names as Reveire and Reviere, as well as Paul Rivoire, he chose the name Revere, a name, his son Paul said, the "*rustres*," or local bumpkins, could better pronounce. He chose a common first name for his son, and Paul neither spoke, wrote, nor read French. Some of these methods of assimilation are common for all immigrants, of course, but the Huguenots' approach was much more swift and radical since they feared detection and possible reprisals by the Catholic Church. So successful were these methods that there was little trace of their origins one or two generations later.

On the first floor in the Paul Revere Banquet Hall is a portrait of Paul himself. It is a copy by Jane Stuart of the original done in 1813 by her father, the famous portrait painter Gilbert Stuart. On the second floor is a bronze replica of the sign which hung over the door of the Green Dragon Tavern where the Massachusetts Masons held their first meeting in 1769; Revere often attended meetings here. On the third floor a replica of a carving from the sign of the Bunch of Grapes Tavern, formerly on King Street (now State Street), is outside the Grand Lodge room. The original was carved from wood that was part of the U.S.S. *Constitution*. In the adjacent Corinthian Hall, a portrait of Lafayette is above the Statue of Charity; as the Masonic lodge information brochure expresses it, he "exchanged the pleasures of life for the perils of the service of an oppressed people."

The Masonic apron worn by General Lafayette and the silver trowel he used at the laying of the cornerstone of the Bunker Hill Monument on June 17, 1825, can be seen by making an appointment with the Grand Secretary at 617-426-6040. Revere's original handwritten speech for the cornerstone ceremonies at the Bunker Hill Monument and a gold urn Revere made which contains a lock of George Washington's hair may also be seen by appointment. The Masonic Temple is open Monday to Friday. There is no fee for entrance and the building is handicapped accessible.

Nearby at the corner of Tremont Street and Boylston Street at the Little Building at **80 Boylston Street** is the site of the former **Hotel Pelham,** the first use in the United States of the "French flat" (with the possible exception of New Orleans). Most British and American houses at the time were vertical residences called townhouses, which had a few rooms on each floor and extended upwards for three or more floors. In contrast, the new flats used widely in France were all on one floor and were quite extensive. Boston was a good site for "French flats" since it was one of the most densely populated American cities, and these flats became popular here, especially in the Back Bay. According to the 1885 edition of *King's Handbook of Boston*, a French flat is "a single tenement occupying the whole or part of a floor, instead of several floors in a house." The word tenement as we now think of it (a rundown, low-rental apartment building) does not apply to these middle- and upper-class dwellings including as many as seven bedrooms, two baths, a kitchen, and service areas. Complete living was the motto. Many of these buildings had restaurants and maid service as well as the standard luxury additions of elevators, private bathrooms, central heating, twenty-four-hour telephone service, and many other amenities. Wags of the day referred to these apartment hotels as being fit for "the newly wed and the nearly dead."

When Tremont Street was widened, the hotel was put on rollers and moved in its entirety, to the amazement of passers-by. This prompted a saying in Cambridge about Boston: "You'd better get up early before the houses begin to move."

The **Boston Conservatory of Music** was located farther west on Boylston Street from this intersection, but records of its original location were lost in a fire. The Conservatory is of interest because one of the teachers there in the late 1800s and early 1900s was a French Canadian named **Calixa Lavallée.** Lavallée composed the Canadian national anthem and, while he was in Boston, in 1891, wrote the music for another important song, *Restons Français,* or "Let's Stay French." He was concerned as were many French Canadians at the time that they would lose their cultural identity if they continued to imitate American ways and choose American values over their own.

As you leave this walk, take your newly found awareness for things French with you. You'll be surprised by what else you will discover. *Bonne chance!* Good Luck!

Old State House

WATERFRONT & VICINITY

*Markets and
Revolutionary Brew*

─────── ⟨ **SETTING THE STAGE** ⟩ ───────

Walk Two's focus on the waterfront and adjacent down-town evokes images of the French role in the American Revolution and the early days of the new republic. It was a third-generation Huguenot, James Bowdoin II, who read the Declaration of Independence from the balcony of the Old State House in 1776, just a hundred years from the date his grandfather had entered Boston Harbor. In 1778, French admiral Count d'Estaing and his naval troops, newly arrived from France to help the colonies, paraded triumphantly down State Street to the Old State House. General Washington's 1789 pro-cession to honor John Hancock, the new governor of Massachusetts, followed the same route. French naval troops were in Washington's procession, too, a power-ful reminder of the strong alliance with France.

MAP OF WALK TWO

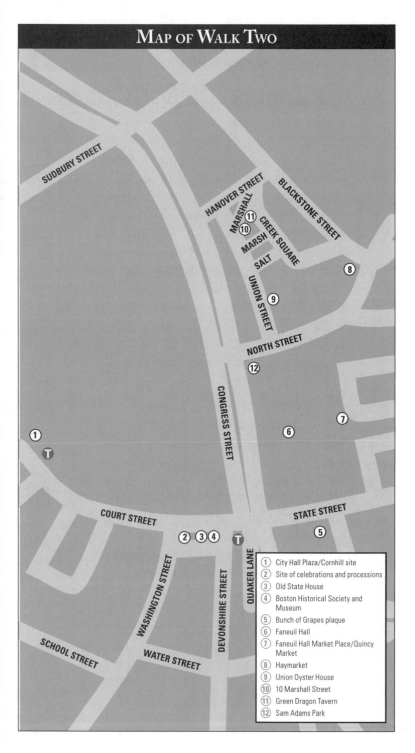

① City Hall Plaza/Cornhill site
② Site of celebrations and processions
③ Old State House
④ Boston Historical Society and Museum
⑤ Bunch of Grapes plaque
⑥ Faneuil Hall
⑦ Faneuil Hall Market Place/Quincy Market
⑧ Haymarket
⑨ Union Oyster House
⑩ 10 Marshall Street
⑪ Green Dragon Tavern
⑫ Sam Adams Park

The taverns once dotting the waterfront were settings for exchanges of information about the Revolution by such men as Huguenot descendant Paul Revere. Although none of these taverns remains, you will see a new version of the Green Dragon Tavern at its new site at 11 Marshall Street. Also on Marshall Street at number 10 is the building where Ebenezer Hancock, deputy paymaster general of the Continental army, stored French coins brought by French ships to pay American troops and buy supplies. In 1789, a French newspaper, the *Courier de Boston*, was published in nearby Cornhill to promote the exchange of goods and services between France and the new republic.

General Lafayette's appearance in the United States in 1824 through 1825 was the scene of much rejoicing and gratitude for the part he had played in the Revolution, especially in Boston. You can see memorabilia manufactured for this famous visit at the Bostonian Society's museum at the Old State House.

Faneuil Hall in the Dock Square section downtown was a gift in 1742 from Huguenot merchant Peter Faneuil, whom we met in Walk One. It was enlarged to its present form in 1805 by Charles Bulfinch and originally had market stalls selling meat, cheese, and other foodstuffs on its ground level.

❦ THE WALK ❦

The plaza around the City Hall is a good place to imagine the Boston of the past, with bustling vendors and hawkers and full of the aromas of salt air, codfish, molasses, and spices. This was **Cornhill,** an extension of today's Washington Street during the years after the American Revolution. It was the main street of Boston and a principal area for residences and businesses

①

alike. Abbé Robin, a French cleric who accompanied the army of Count Rochambeau in Boston during the American Revolution, observed the harbor's mercantile scene in the late eighteenth century. He reported that codfish was the Bostonian's principal article of commerce, and that they preferred Madeira or Oporto sherries to French wines, but usually drank rum which was distilled from molasses which they obtained in the "islands."

Imagine "newspaper row" here in 1789 with bookstores and bookstalls and printing offices. It was at Samuel Hall's at **53 the Cornhill** that the new republic's first newspaper printed in French was for sale. The French weekly *Courier de Boston*, costing five pence, was a unique and far-reaching periodical with utopian goals and dreams. Its editor was the Frenchman Joseph Nancrède, a French teacher at Harvard College and a bookseller, who was eager to promote commercial and cultural exchange between the United States, the new democracy, and Europe, particularly France.

Nancrède viewed America as a vast and fertile land with well-cultivated fields assuring the country a forever-expanding commerce extending not only to Europe, but also to the East and West Indies. It needs a universal communication, he felt, as universal as the commerce itself. Clearly, the French language would be ideal for such communication, since it is spoken in all parts of Europe and wherever the Americans would take their commerce. Thus, the study of French in America should be encouraged. Also, the universal use of French would enable a presentation of the politics, arts, and sciences as well as the commerce of the new country for the interest of the navigator, negotiator, cultivator, and the politician.

Notices of ship arrivals and advertisements for recently arrived goods and domestic wares were included in each edition. One issue also gave the results of the recent American elections. To further educate his readers, Nancrède offered notes from Warsaw, Vienna, Smyrna, Berlin, England, France, and the United States, state by state. An account of the first session of the new American Congress is included. At the close of each edition the price in shillings of articles obtainable in Boston are listed; a gallon of Madeira costs 9 to 14 shillings, for example. The edition ends with reports of the stock exchanges in the United States, and London, Paris, Amsterdam, and other major cities worldwide. The paper was available in large American cities, the French islands, and France.

Evidently, his readers were somewhat fickle, for at one point Nancrède made the following appeal: "We are not ignorant of the fact that the taste of the century demands more spice, more things shocking. There are so few persons who read to be instructed. The *Courier de Boston*, which has need of encouragement, does not have recourse to the methods usually practiced." Unfortunately, the encouragement and readers eager for instruction did not appear; the periodical lasted only six months. Its invitation to the new republic to join French-based European-American commerce was far ahead of its time. Copies of the newspaper can be seen at the Boston Athenaeum, described in Walk Four.

We next see M. Nancrède of Williams Court proposing a French day school for boys ages eleven to fifteen in the paper the *Massachusetts Centinel*. To remove any doubts in their parents' minds as to his ability, he promises to perfect every pupil's French who attends his institution for two years without interruption. Worldwide service in this new era would require training in French for Boston's future statesmen and merchants.

Where **State Street** met the head of **Washington Street** was the site of many celebrations and processions. This was the end of the main route into Boston by land along Boston Neck, a narrow strip of land which connected the peninsula of Boston to the mainland. It was also the end of the route from the harbor via State Street.

In 1778 **Admiral Count d'Estaing**, commander of the fleet sent from France to assist the Revolutionary cause, made a splendid entry with his troops from their waterfront landing down State Street, ending at the Old State House.

This was also the scene in October 1789 of a triumphant procession honoring **George Washington**. Weeks after becoming president of the United States, Washington came to Boston for the inauguration of John Hancock as the first governor of the Commonwealth of Massachusetts. French naval officers were given the place of honor in the parade, preceded only by town officials, magistrates, and consuls.

Testifying to the new republic's democratic nature, after clergy, lawyers, merchants, and various marine cadres, came forty-six alphabetized lots of artisans and tradesmen, then numerous seamen. The procession was enlivened by the French troops marching to a band made up of several kinds of instruments, in contrast with the simple American fife and drum.

Excitement was even higher in August of 1824 when **General Lafayette** returned to Boston for the city's largest celebration in its history for this favorite old friend. He had been invited to be a guest of the United States for a year's tour of the entire country in 1824 and 1825.

He entered the post-Revolutionary city via the same route as Washington some thirty-five years earlier. Thousands turned out to see Lafayette. Boston's Light Infantry, marching with a cavalcade of twelve hundred horsemen, greeted him at the Neck where Boston proper began. Lafayette rode in an open barouche pulled by four white horses. When he reached the center of Boston he was greeted by cannons, bells, and the heartfelt cries of his adopted countrymen. It had been forty years since he had borrowed money from American shopkeepers to buy shoes for his troops.

The **Old State House** at **206 Washington Street**, built ③ in 1713 and rebuilt in 1748, is a graceful red brick building ornamented by gold pre-Revolutionary symbols of a lion and a unicorn flanking the façade at the balcony end of its gambrel roof. The building now houses the **Boston Historical Society**, its museum, and a gift ④ shop which can be entered on the right side of the building.

Old State House

The museum contains artifacts from Lafayette's 1824–1825 tour of the United States, such as commemorative textiles, ceramic pieces, and medals. The widespread sale of these items throughout the country is evidence of Lafayette's great popularity with the American public. The collection includes a pair of women's white leather gloves and a sash with Lafayette's portrait on them worn to the 1825 reception for Lafayette. During his visit and even after he left, women wore accessories with his likeness on them to show their appreciation of Boston's hero. A ceramic pitcher decorated with Lafayette and George Washington's images and a tablecloth and napkin from the Bunker Hill dedication banquet are also in the museum's collection.

Bunch of Grapes Tavern plaque

The museum is open daily, with a small admission fee. The first floor is wheelchair accessible.

The Old State House is of interest to Francophiles for another reason. When you go past the museum entrance follow the Freedom Trail's double brick line in the sidewalk until you reach the other side of Congress Street. Look back at the rear of the State House and its balcony.

On July 18, 1776, as church bells rang and boats saluted in the harbor in celebration of the signing of the Declaration of Independence, **James Bowdoin II**, Harvard graduate, twice governor of Massachusetts, and descendant of Huguenot émigrés, gave the first public reading of the Declaration of Independence from the balcony. The date, 1776, was exactly one hundred years from the time that his Huguenot grandfather, Pierre Baudouin, entered Boston harbor. Such was the speed and silence of the French assimilation in Boston. (More information about the Bowdoin family is in Walk Four.)

⑤ A popular Whig tavern, the **Bunch of Grapes**, was found at the southeast corner of **State and Kilby streets**;

Whigs supported the war against England during the American Revolution. It was here that Lafayette was received with honors on his return from France in 1784. Many other patriots frequented this tavern, including Paul Revere and Samuel Adams. The Bunch of Grapes was also the scene of the first meeting of the Masons' Provincial Grand Lodge in Massachusetts in 1733.

The many taverns in this area in pre-Revolutionary times served as clubs for men, meeting places where the news could be heard, a bed could be found (some taverns doubled as inns), and, of course, a convivial drink could be shared. It is interesting to note that in colonial Boston, if a woman lost her husband, she was given a license to open a rum shop. There seemed to be one on every corner!

Here among the former taverns the eating habits of the colonials might be considered, the common diet before French cuisine insinuated itself into a few daring Boston restaurants. Cured pork was the biggest staple for these hearty men and women, pork fed by the abundant New England crops of corn. Fresh meat was seldom prepared. At first an open hearth was sufficient for cooking; the safer and more efficient fireplace and Rumford stove soon replaced the hearth.

Food styles changed rapidly after the Revolution. A nineteenth-century cookbook by a Mrs. Lee claimed that the status of cook should be equal to that of a physician. She felt that dyspepsia, or indigestion, a common complaint of the period, was caused by a diet high in fat and low in fiber. Reformer and author Mary Peabody, better known as Mrs. Horace Mann, wife of the Boston educator, wrote that taste was given by God. These more sophisticated notions about food and taste brought the young nation closer to a French appreciation of cuisine.

⑥ **Faneuil Hall** was a gift of Peter Faneuil, a wealthy Huguenot merchant who inherited his fortune from his uncle, André Faneuil of La Rochelle, France. (See Walk One for more information about the Faneuils.) It took more than one vote for the town officials to accept this magnificent gift. Could this resistance be because Faneuil was a foreigner—particularly, a French foreigner?

Faneuil Hall

The building was constructed in 1740–42 by John Smibert, with assembly rooms above and an open market below, much like European market buildings. Perhaps Faneuil directed Smibert to make the hall as much like a French market building as possible. Restored under Charles Bulfinch in 1805, the building was doubled in width, the height of the Assembly Hall was raised, and a third floor was added.

To learn more about this building and the Faneuils, go to the rear of Faneuil Hall to a stairway leading to the upper floors. Free presentations are given here throughout the day by well-informed National Park Rangers.

⑦ Directly across from the rear of Faneuil Hall you will find the **Faneuil Hall Market Place**, or **Quincy Market**. This successful urban renewal project—in both the 1820s and the 1970s—was named after its originator Josiah Quincy, mayor of Boston from 1823 to 1828.

The rectangular granite warehouses for grain and other foodstuffs, designed in the Greek Revival style by architect Alexander Parris, were built on newly made land at the Town Dock in 1824–26. A century and a half later, in 1976-78, the rundown buildings were adapted for reuse as a "festival market," by Benjamin Thompson and Associates, the first such project in the United States and an immensely successful one, now imitated widely. The center warehouse, Quincy Market, was converted into a food court and the North and South Market buildings on either side are filled with shops, restaurants, and boutiques. New buildings were added to the rear of the complex.

Au Bon Pain on Boylston Street near Berkeley Street

A Boston landmark, the **Au Bon Pain** chain of cafés began here in 1978, when owner Louis Kane opened a French yogurt stand at Quincy Market. Next, he imported French bakers to teach the proper use of French ovens and how to bake French breads and pastries. After a few months the chefs returned to France, and Au Bon Pain was launched. Au Bon Pain breads have won several informal competitions with French products held by French bakers. The cafés now serve all kinds of bakery goods, soups, sandwiches, and salads in several locations in Boston, throughout the United States, and internationally.

Each Friday and Saturday you will find another kind of market along Blackstone Street and around the corner on North Street, the outdoor **Haymarket**. This traditional outdoor market originated at the turn of the century, then as now predominantly Italian. Often the stalls pass from father to son.

⑧

In the narrow alleys crowded with stalls, it is hard to tell which is more colorful: the stacks of shiny eggplants and tomatoes, the rows of tropical fruits, or

the bright clothes and diverse languages of the shoppers. The stands at the corner of Blackstone and North streets specialize in food from the French West Indies, so be prepared for people in exotic dress originally from Guadeloupe, Martinique, or Haiti

Haymarket

buying plantains, cilantro, and mangoes and probably speaking French. Throughout the market you might also hear French from France, Morocco, or Senegal, as well as Cantonese, Mandarin, Vietnamese, Arabic, Russian, Spanish, German, and, of course, Italian.

Haymarket has its regulars who are there very early each weekend for their bargains and chats with their favorite dealers. Don't forget to dicker and especially don't forget to laugh and joke—they're both part of market tradition the world over. Open-air markets are better known in the rest of the world than in the United States, where our supermarkets offer Muzak, plastic-wrapped food, and impersonal service instead of a sensual and nourishing experience.

The market is open Fridays and Saturdays, starting about daybreak. Some stands are open all week. Prices are very low, especially on Saturday night when the vendors are packing up to go home and want to carry as little as possible with them.

In the mid-1700s the waterfront came to the back door of the shops along Union Street, though otherwise so little has changed since colonial days in the area of Union and Marshall with its cobblestone streets and old buildings that it is called the "Attic of Boston."

Stop at **41 Union Street**, a low building with a brick upper story and wooden first floor, the **Union Oyster House**. An oyster bar and restaurant since 1826, before that it was a shop selling fine dress goods and textiles. In the late eighteenth century, it belonged to James Amblard, a Frenchman by birth, who lived on the second floor over the shop. When the **Duc de Chartres**—later **King Louis Philippe of France**—was exiled and came to America in 1796, he visited Boston for a while and lived with the Amblard family at 41 Union Street. (Some accounts say he lived with a family named Capen at that same address.) Both reports agree that he earned money teaching French to young men eager to enter the new French-American business opportunities and to fashionable young girls and

⑨

Union Oyster House

ladies as well. The Duc de Chartres and his brother
traveled extensively throughout the eastern states until
their mother and advisors thought it was time for their
return.

The young Duc de Chartres frequently played chess
with a Mr. Fowle at the Amblard home, according to
a long-preserved family story. On the Duc's departure
to London in 1800, he left a set of chessmen to Fowle,
which was preserved by the family, giving credence to
their account. The Duc became King Louis Philippe in
1830 and reigned until his abdication in 1848.

Around the corner at **10 Marshall Street** is a
modest brick building dating back to the eighteenth
century. Here Deputy Paymaster General of the
Continental army **Ebenezer Hancock** carried out his
duties; the wide plank floors were loaded with trunks
and bags of French coins on loan from Louis XVI, sent
to Boston in guarded flotillas of ships. These French
funds enabled the colonists to continue their battle. A
double ring of armed soldiers circled the building to
protect one large shipment of two million silver crowns
destined to win the colonists' victory.

11 Marshall Street is the present home of the **Green Dragon Tavern**, formerly on the site of the nearby Holocaust Memorial. The original Green Dragon, a mansion built in the mid-1600s, was called the "headquarters of the Revolution" by statesman Daniel Webster. (The British, on the other hand, called the tavern a "nest of treason.") It became the meeting place of the "Sons of Liberty," a radical group of patriots. Many of the men who gathered here participated in the Boston Tea Party, including Huguenot descendant Paul Revere. Half a century after the Revolution, however, the building was destroyed when Union Street was widened.

At **Sam Adams Park** as you face Faneuil Hall, you'll find a marker to your left labeled Town Dock at **Dock Square**. A dock once here connected the town with the harbor where the deeper waters lay. Benches nearby now invite you to sit down and read some tales about the French and the sea.

Tales abound about the French navy and their part in the American Revolution. The colonists' navy, established only in 1775, was so inexperienced that French naval aid was an enormous asset and played a critical part in the colonists' victory.

French preparation for the coming conflict was in full operation by 1776. Arms shipments from France and the West Indies were picked up by colonial rebels along the East Coast to avoid seizure by the British in Boston Harbor; sometimes false French papers would disguise the identity of an American ship. The French opened their ports to American gunrunners and privateers. Battalions of French infantry were moved to the

West Indies and a French naval squadron began training maneuvers for the coming war.

In May 1776, the French Royal Council decided to aid Americans with money for munitions and to prepare the French fleet for combat; this was the first formal decision concerning France's role in the war. It was a Huguenot, Jacques Le Ray de Chaumont of Nantes in France, who sent the gift of a large ship containing cannon powder to Boston; this was carried overland to win the crucial Saratoga campaign in 1777, a victory which helped persuade the king of France of the colonists' ability to win the war. (Count Le Ray de Chaumont was awarded acres of rather stony, hilly ground in eastern Pennsylvania and extensive land in upstate New York for his aid.) In February of 1778 France signed a treaty with the colonies recognizing them as an independent country and pledging to be "a good and faithful ally," and officially entered the war.

That April a royal French fleet of warships, twelve ships of the line and five frigates under the command of Admiral Count d'Estaing, left Toulon in southeastern France for the colonies. They landed at Narragansett Bay in July to fight in a British attack on Newport, Rhode Island. However, a gale dispersed them to sea and they sailed to Boston for repairs and treatment of the wounded. The Chevalier Joseph Louis de Raimondis lost an arm in this battle, saying, "I am ready to lose my other arm in the cause of the Americas."

Admiral Count d'Estaing presented a figure of strength and reassurance to the beleaguered colonists. He was adept at smoothing over difficult situations between his men and the citizens of Boston and developed a mutually supportive relationship with George Washington. Initially, Washington was somewhat in awe of this aristocrat and accomplished military leader, but their relationship soon grew to one of friendship.

In a letter of July 1778, at d'Estaing's arrival, Washington wrote, "Sir, I take the liberty, in behalf of the United States to present you with a small quantity of livestock; which I flatter myself after a long sea voyage may not be unacceptable." In a later letter Washington said the arrival of the fleet "belonging to his most Christian Majesty on our coast is an event that makes me truly happy and permit me to observe that the pleasure I feel upon the occasion is greatly increased by the command being placed in a gentleman of such distinguished talents, experience, reputation as the Count d'Estaing."

During d'Estaing's stay, John Hancock gave an extravagant ball at Boston's Concert Hall in his honor. Admiral d'Estaing was later made a member of the Society of the Cincinnati, founded in the United States in 1783 and established in France soon after. The society was named for Lucius Quinctius Cincinnatus, a fifth-century BC Roman called from farming his fields to lead his country. Commissioned officers in the Continental and French army and navy were eligible for membership.

During the war, French ships guarded the port of Boston; also, many ships in need of repair and refitting were anchored in Boston's inner harbor. Other, bigger ships—ranging from ninety guns down to twenty-six guns—were stationed in Nantasket Roads just outside Boston Harbor.

These ships and their navy were of great interest to the Bostonians. Of course, most Boston citizens had never met a French person. Their ideas and opinions about the French had come largely from the British, not known for their love of the French. Thus curiosity, gratitude, misconception, and suspicion informed the colonists' response to the French crew and officers. Even men of education and social standing sometimes believed the generally negative views of the French held by the British, reinforced by generations-old memories of the French and Indian wars and of the vast French territories in Canada.

Commander Chevalier de Sainneville described a festive dinner welcoming the French officers of the frigate *La Nymphe*, the first of the fleet to arrive. "One enthusiastic person after having taken something to drink, threw his arms around my neck in his rapture at seeing me in their midst. He congratulated me on being on the first warship of the King of France seen in Boston and forced me to agree with him that my situation was an epoch-making one."

Another story perhaps should be taken with some reservations. In his *Recollections*, published in 1877, merchant, politician, and Boston resident Samuel Breck reported on the result of the almost universal conception that Frenchmen lived on salad and frogs. When the first squadron arrived in Boston, the townspeople flocked to the wharves to see the Frenchmen presumably skinny from such a diet, but were surprised at the portly officers and vigorous sailors. A Mr. Tracy, wealthy resident of Cambridge, invited the admiral and his officers to a great feast at his large villa there. At dinner two large tureens of soup were placed at the ends of the table. Admiral Count d'Estaing sat on the right of Tracy, and Monsieur de l'Etombe, the Consul of France, sat on the left. When l'Etombe put his spoon in the tureen, he fished up a large frog, "just as green and perfect as if he had hopped from the pond into the tureen." He exclaimed, *"Ah, mon Dieu! une grenouille!"* ("Oh, my God, a frog!") and passed it around for the laughing company to see. When the servants served each guest with a soup plate with a frog floating in it, the merriment was complete. Tracy, however, was dismayed that the frogs so carefully caught in the swamps of Cambridge that morning proved not to be the national dish of France.

Other Frenchmen also showed their support for the American cause. **Louis Ansart de Marequelle** came to aid the colonies in the winter of 1776, offering to construct furnaces to build iron cannons by a new process he had invented. His proposition was gratefully accepted; the newly formed fighting troops needed more weapons. He also supervised the defense of buildings in Boston Harbor as well as the protection of Admiral Count d'Estaing's ships.

Much of the drama of the conflict between the struggling colonies and England was set in the busy, narrow streets and shops and taverns of the waterfront and downtown area sampled by this walk. The role of French support for the young country is particularly evident here. Yet the importance of the monumental aid given by the French to the colonies before, during, and after the Revolution has been minimized by the United States. This unwillingness to acknowledge the significance of French help is perhaps a reluctance on the part of the United States to admit that the war could not be won alone. It is also the result, possibly, of lingering religious prejudices between Protestants and Catholics, and of the American suspicion of things French.

This walk should inspire a deeper appreciation of the French presence in Boston as well as gratitude for their generous assistance to the emerging nation.

United Shoe Machinery Building

FINANCIAL DISTRICT

*Old Money and
Art Deco Treasures*

❧ SETTING THE STAGE ❧

Walk Three covers Boston's financial district, the
oldest in the United States, and offers a collection of
surprising French connections encompassing monarchs
and revolutionaries, priests and Protestants, as well as
cuisine and architecture. General Lafayette toasted the
young republic at a dinner in his honor in 1824 at the
Exchange Coffee House on the site now occupied by
One Exchange Place. You can use your imagination to
visualize Boston's celebration at Liberty Square in 1793
in honor of the French Revolution.

A French restaurant once in this area, "Julien's
Restorator," educated the palates of Bostonians as
early as 1794. The Langham Hotel Boston at 250
Franklin Street, part of the French Meridien Group,
features Julien's Restaurant, named after the early
restaurant owner. The walk also visits the site of the

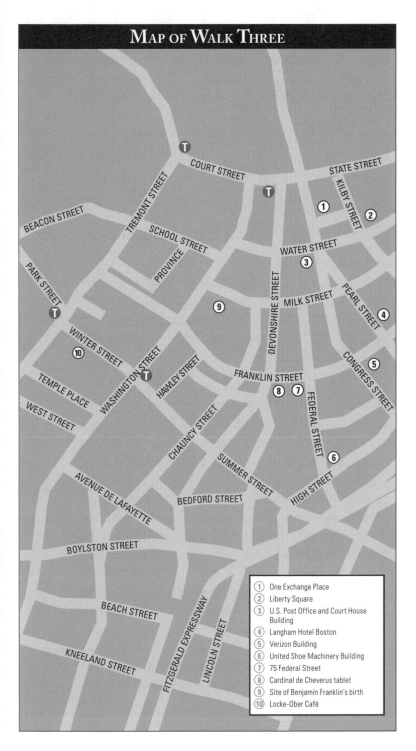

MAP OF WALK THREE

COURT STREET

STATE STREET

KILBY STREET

TREMONT STREET

BEACON STREET

SCHOOL STREET

① One Exchange Place

② Liberty Square

PROVINCE

WATER STREET

③

PARK STREET

DEVONSHIRE STREET

MILK STREET

PEARL STREET

④

⑨

WINTER STREET

⑤

CONGRESS STREET

⑩

WASHINGTON STREET

HAWLEY STREET

FRANKLIN STREET

⑧ ⑦

TEMPLE PLACE

FEDERAL STREET

WEST STREET

CHAUNCY STREET

⑥

SUMMER STREET

AVENUE DE LAFAYETTE

BEDFORD STREET

HIGH STREET

BOYLSTON STREET

BEACH STREET

FITZGERALD EXPRESSWAY

LINCOLN STREET

KNEELAND STREET

① One Exchange Place
② Liberty Square
③ U.S. Post Office and Court House Building
④ Langham Hotel Boston
⑤ Verizon Building
⑥ United Shoe Machinery Building
⑦ 75 Federal Street
⑧ Cardinal de Cheverus tablet
⑨ Site of Benjamin Franklin's birth
⑩ Locke-Ober Café

former residence of Jean Lefebvre de Cheverus, a priest who fled from France and arrived in Boston in 1796 after refusing to support the French Revolution's Civil Constitution of the Clergy. He did much to create peace between Boston Protestants and Roman Catholics.

Benjamin Franklin was born here at former 17 Milk Street, now One Milk Street. A friend of the French, Franklin was successful in persuading them to be an ally in the American Revolution. A jewelry store at former 11 Milk Street was operated continuously by the Johonnot family of Huguenot ancestry from the 1600s until 1958.

The Art Deco buildings in the financial district were built mostly in the 1920s and 1930s in the French *Arts Décoratifs* style. Examples include the Post Office Building at Congress Street, the Verizon Building, and the United Shoe Machinery Building (the influential first Art Deco skyscraper built in Boston 1928–30). The outstanding Art Deco buildings at 75 and 101 Federal Street are a 1929 original and a 1988 copy harmoniously combined.

———————— ❦ **THE WALK** ❧ ————————

At **One Exchange Place** at **53 State Street** stood the ① **Exchange Coffee House**. Very tall for its day, the seven-story extravaganza built from plans by American architect Asher Benjamin had cost half a million dollars at its completion in 1808, after two and a half years of construction. This "coffee house" contained more than two hundred apartments and a dining room seating three hundred people. It was at the center of a teeming business area, and was the stopping place for stagecoaches entering or leaving the town. Its life was short, however, for it burned ten years later. The rebuilt coffee house was somewhat less grandiose, but was nevertheless the site of a dinner celebrating General Lafayette's visit to Boston in 1824. At this occasion he gave the following toast: "The city of Boston, the cradle of liberty; may Faneuil Hall ever stand a monument to teach the world that resistance to oppression is a duty, and will, under true republic institutions, become a blessing."

Nearby in the former **Congress Square** near **Hawes Street** was the printing office of the newspaper *Colombian Centinel*, established in 1784. It was here that the young **Duc de Chartres**, later King Louis Philippe of France, came to submit his articles for publication. He was invaluable since he was able to show the editor an atlas in his possession, which illustrated with great accuracy the location of the battlefields in the current war between France and a combined Europe. The *Centinel* could then scoop its contemporaries by giving its readers the latest topographical information.

Another visitor to the offices, it is said, was **Louis Napoleon**, later emperor of France as Napoleon III. It is ironic that Napoleon I's nephew, Louis Napoleon, was the beneficiary of the revolution of 1848 which unseated King Louis Philippe, bringing the fate of these two men full circle.

② **Liberty Square**, at the intersection of **Kilby and Water streets,** was named for the sixty-foot liberty pole erected at the end of the eighteenth century to commemorate the Stamp Act riots that had taken place

here in 1765. (A liberty pole was a flagstaff display-
ing a liberty cap or flag or other symbol of resistance.)
In addition, when the news of the French Revolution
reached Boston on January 24, 1793, a gigantic civic
feast and noisy celebration was held on this spot to
rejoice in the freedom of their
French brothers and sisters.
An ox was roasted on Copp's
Hill in the North End and
its horns, the symbol of aristocracy, were carried through
the streets atop a sixty-foot
pole and then triumphantly
raised in the square. A fif-
teen-gun salute was fired.
Entertainment was provided
during the afternoon at
Faneuil Hall, presided over
by Samuel Adams. Tables
then were laid from one end

Liberty Square

of the old State Street to Kilby Street for the roast ox
and other food. Liberty and Equality were extolled
and toasted and the singing and dancing continued
long into the night.

Another tribute to freedom was erected in the
square in the 1980s, a statue honoring the October
1956 Hungarian Revolution.

French statesman and diplomat **Charles Maurice de
Talleyrand-Perigord**, better known as **Talleyrand**,
lived with a Mr. William Lee on Water Street. He
visited the nearby studio of Gilbert Stuart, painter of
George Washington's portrait. The artist immediately

sized up the Frenchman: "If that man is not a villain, the Almighty does not write with a legible hand." A man capable of playing several sides of the game, Talleyrand was according to many invaluable in obtaining France as an ally in the Revolutionary War, yet later sent French ships to capture American vessels in the "Quasi-War," an undeclared war fought entirely at sea between the United States and France from 1798 to 1801.

(3) The **U.S. Post Office and Court House** at the corner of Water and Congress streets is a very good example of the Art Deco style. Geometric designs and stylized

U.S. Post Office and Court House

plant forms ornament the façade; the windows are recessed slits. The term "Art Deco" is derived from the French term *Arts Décoratifs* from the *Exposition Internationale des Arts Décoratifs et Industriels Modernes* held in Paris in 1925. In vogue between 1925 and 1940, the style is characterized by streamlined shapes and stylized designs. Although Boston has several good examples of Art Deco buildings, the style was not as popular in Boston or Philadelphia as it was in New York City, Miami, Los Angeles, and Chicago.

Next in the area of the Post Office you will be near the location of the first French restaurant in Boston, **Julien's Restorator**, which is said to have coaxed Boston's palate into submission. It was located on part of the present **Post Office** site on Congress Street at Angell Memorial Park. After the French Revolution, **Jean Baptiste Gilbert Payplat**, also called **Julien**, left France for Boston. (Some accounts say he came here via Martinique, where he was cook to a French gentleman.) In 1794 he bought the Bridgman house off Milk Street, then owned by a leather dresser or tanner. The wooden-gabled house, known afterwards as Julien's Restorator, was a place of popular entertainment and good French food until Julien's death in 1805. According to legend, his wife carried on as the chef in secret for a few years after his death.

At **Pearl and Franklin streets** you will find the **Langham Hotel Boston**, part of the **French Hotel Meridien** group. Formerly a Federal Reserve bank, its transformation into a hotel is an excellent example of adaptive reuse. The Langham Hotel's dining room is named **Julien's**, the menu featuring French food, appropriately.

④

Farther down **Pearl Street**, though outside the confines of this walk, is the site of a dramatic (if unverified) story featuring **George Washington Lafayette**, General Lafayette's son. Soon after the French Revolution, a very wealthy resident of Pearl Street, **Thomas Handasyd Perkins**, a Boston merchant mentioned in Walk One, was in Paris with a friend, where he was introduced to Lafayette's wife. She was in great distress: General Lafayette was in prison in Paris since his views were at odds with the new government and their son had been conscripted into the French military. Madame

Lafayette feared their son would not be well treated because of his father's role during the French Revolution. At her request, Perkins and his friend obtained forged papers so that the younger Lafayette, in disguise, could leave France and live with the Perkins family on Pearl Street until it was safe for him to return.

Verizon Building detail

At **185 Franklin Street** is another excellent example of Art Deco. Now Verizon headquarters, the building was designed in 1947 by the long-standing Boston architectural firm Cram and Ferguson. If you would like to see more Art Deco buildings, turn left on Congress and go down to High Street where you will turn right to find the **United Shoe Machinery Building** at **High Street at 138–164 Federal Street.** It was the first Art Deco skyscraper built in Boston and influenced future buildings of this type in both Boston and New York. The base is composed of black granite and limestone and the building is covered in metal, brick, and stone. The various vertical blocks step back progressively until a single cap is reached at the top of the building. You can see the original Art Deco metalwork in the lobby, which is still intact.

The outstanding 1929 Art Deco building at **75 Federal Street** was joined to **101 Federal Street**, built in the Art Deco style in 1988, to great effect. The

(5)

(6)

(7)

original Art Deco lobby at 75 Federal Street has been preserved; the golden and black marble and "Broadway Engraved" lettering make a striking combination.

On the face of **76 Franklin Street** between **Federal Street and Devonshire Street** you will find a tablet dedicated to the **Most Reverend Jean L.A.M. Lefebvre de Cheverus**, Boston's first Catholic bishop, who lived in this vicinity. De Cheverus arrived in Boston in the summer of 1796, having fled France in fear of his life for refusing to support the harsh Civil Constitution of the Clergy instituted during the French Revolution. (The French generally do not emigrate unless subjected to very difficult conditions.) Father Matignon, a former school acquaintance and at that time a pastor in Boston, invited young de Cheverus, known already as an aristocrat and a scholar, to seek refuge in Boston.

(8)

Jean Lefebvre de Cheverus

Part of his early ministry was with the Indians in Maine, who loved him deeply. (Maine was still part of the state of Massachusetts at that time.) De Cheverus became active in the Boston of his day, and popular among Catholics and Protestants alike, no small achievement. It was said of him that he "possessed that French politeness and delicacy of manners." As a scholar, he was a member of the elite Anthology Society and donated many books to the club, which was later to become the **Boston Athenaeum Library** at 10½ Beacon Street. The Anthology Society listed among its members lawyer and political writer John Lowell, Boston mayors Josiah Quincy and Harrison Gray Otis, and Rev. John Thornton Kirkland, president of Harvard. Many years later, the Athenaeum deemed de Cheverus "France's greatest gift to the spiritual life of Boston."

ON THIS SITE STOOD THE RESIDENCE OF
JEAN LEFEBVRE DECHEVERUS
FIRST ROMAN CATHOLIC BISHOP
OF BOSTON
BELOVED BY PROTESTANT AND CATHOLIC ALIKE
BORN IN FRANCE 1768
MADE BISHOP 1808
RECALLED TO FRANCE IN 1823
LATER MADE CARDINAL ARCHBISHOP
OF BORDEAUX WHERE HE DIED IN 1836
"HIS THOUGHTS WERE AS A PYRAMID UPHELD
ON WHOSE FAR TOP AN ANGEL STOOD AND SMILED
YET IN HIS HEART HE WAS A CHILD"
THIS TABLET PLACED BY THE CITY OF BOSTON 1925

Cardinal de Cheverus Tablet

By the end of the eighteenth century, France's popularity in America had faded in some quarters; American merchant shipping was a victim of the ongoing and growing conflict between Britain and France. The seizure of American ships in Italy by Napoleon contributed to this animosity as war threatened. Demonstrating his concern not only for his fellow Bostonians but also for the good name of the French, Father de Cheverus and two hundred men of the parish of the newly constructed Catholic Holy Cross Cathedral labored mightily to build up the fortifications at Dorchester Heights to protect their city from British attack, thus earning Father de Cheverus and the Catholics the gratitude of Boston.

De Cheverus was later summoned back to France in spite of long petitions to keep him in Boston, signed by both Catholics and Protestants. He was made an archbishop in France shortly before his death. Many other French priests made outstanding contributions to the growth and development of the Roman Catholic Church in Boston, which are sometimes overshadowed by the greater numbers of Irish clergy in the city's history.

The tablet commemorating de Cheverus reads as follows:

ON THIS SITE STOOD THE RESIDENCE OF

JEAN LEFEBVRE DE CHEVERUS

FIRST ROMAN CATHOLIC BISHOP

OF BOSTON

BELOVED BY PROTESTANT AND CATHOLIC ALIKE

BORN IN FRANCE 1768

MADE BISHOP 1808

RECALLED TO FRANCE IN 1823

LATER MADE CARDINAL ARCHBISHOP

OF BORDEAUX WHERE HE DIED IN 1836

"HIS THOUGHTS WERE AS A PYRAMID UPHELD

ON WHOSE FAR TOP AN ANGEL STOOD AND SMILED

YET IN HIS HEART HE WAS A CHILD"

THIS TABLET PLACED BY THE CITY OF BOSTON 1925

Opposite the Old South Meeting House on **Milk Street** is a building now numbered **One Milk Street,** which formerly contained **17 and 11 Milk Street**. **17 Milk Street** was the site of the simple seventeenth-century wooden house where **Benjamin Franklin**, destined to be a loyal friend to France and to the French, was born in 1706. On the second-floor level of the façade you will find a carved bust of Franklin to the left of the center doorway.

The former **11 Milk Street** was once the home and store of a Huguenot couple, the daughter of **André Sigourney** and **Daniel Johonnot**'s son, a jeweler, as were many Huguenots. The store and living quarters upstairs stayed in the Johonnot family from the seventeenth century through 1958, when Charles W. Johonnot was the owner of a jewelry store on the same spot.

The story of the arrival of the Sigourney family in Boston is typical of Huguenot escapes from France. André Sigourney had lived comfortably near south-western La Rochelle in France until the Edict of

Nantes was revoked in 1685, reducing the already slim civil and religious rights of the Huguenots and increasing their persecution. News of the revocation reached André while he was away from home. He immediately returned and had the luck to see a ship in La Rochelle's harbor bound for England at high tide, a ship already overloaded with cargo and fleeing Huguenots. He ran home, according to the story, and asked his wife

Birthplace of Benjamin Franklin

to choose between allegiance to papal canons or leaving her home that moment. Fortunately, she was of the same persuasion as he and, after putting two suits of clothes on their children to avoid suspicious baggage, they fled to board the waiting vessel. There was no securing of property or packing; they did not even linger long enough, we are told, to eat the Sunday dinner prepared for them.

On **Winter Place**, a narrow alley off Winter Street, is the **Locke-Ober Café**. This unusual location did not stop the owner Louis Ober, a French Alsatian, from

⑩

establishing a gentlemen's restaurant here in 1868. (Women were permitted to dine only in private upstairs rooms.) Soon famous, it was among the first brave Boston restaurants to introduce fine French wines and French food to its clients: truffles, sweetbread, calves' brains, and Madeira souf-flé were not typical fare for mid-nineteenth century Boston. Another Frenchman purchased the restaurant in 1901 and supervised it until his death in 1939.

Locke-Ober Café

Throughout the Victorian era and beyond, Locke-Ober upheld its time-hallowed traditions in cuisine, decor, and the men-only dining room. It was not until the 1980s that women could dine in the downstairs dining room, on special occasions. When the restaurant changed hands late in 2001, the new owner was a woman!

Walk Three ends here; Boston should appear more French with each block. Look for street names and building styles as you walk through the city to see traces of things French.

French Second Empire
Egyptian Revival House

BEACON HILL

Swan Houses and
French West Indies Connections

⟨ SETTING THE STAGE ⟩ ---

Walk Four finds French influences on Beacon Hill in
its personalities and its architecture. Some places will
require your imagination: for example, the site of the
first Catholic Church in Boston with services in French
is now a parking lot. The site is opposite 10½ Beacon
Street, the address of the Boston Athenaeum, a private
library with an extensive collection of books and art,
many French-related.

Your imagination also can recreate the mansion of
third-generation Huguenot James Bowdoin II at the
corner of Beacon and Bowdoin Streets, two-term governor of Massachusetts and a leader in Boston's political
and cultural life. General Lafayette is associated with
a number of sites on this walk as well. In and around
the Massachusetts State House are several reminders of

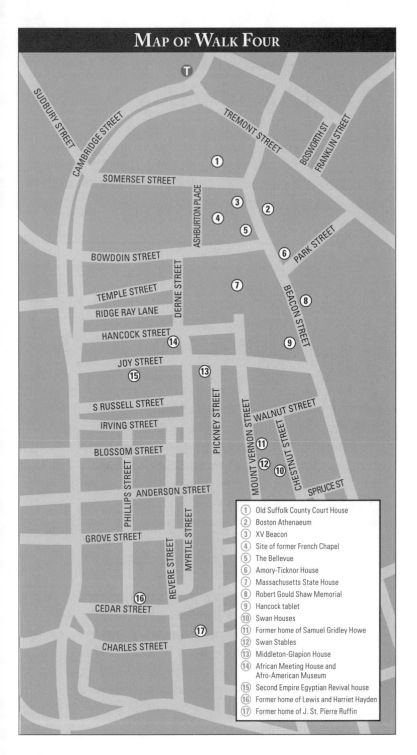

MAP OF WALK FOUR

① Old Suffolk County Court House
② Boston Athenaeum
③ XV Beacon
④ Site of former French Chapel
⑤ The Bellevue
⑥ Amory-Ticknor House
⑦ Massachusetts State House
⑧ Robert Gould Shaw Memorial
⑨ Hancock tablet
⑩ Swan Houses
⑪ Former home of Samuel Gridley Howe
⑫ Swan Stables
⑬ Middleton-Glapion House
⑭ African Meeting House and Afro-American Museum
⑮ Second Empire Egyptian Revival house
⑯ Former home of Lewis and Harriet Hayden
⑰ Former home of J. St. Pierre Ruffin

French and American cooperation, as well as the occasional clash.

French furniture and art inspired the fortunes and misfortunes of the wealthy and unconventional Swan family, as well as gracing their homes—and now the galleries of Boston's Museum of Fine Arts.

Africans taken from their homeland to the French West Indies and on to America were part of the population of Beacon Hill's North Slope, once the heart of Boston's nineteenth-century African-American community.

French architecture aficionados will be rewarded by a rare example of Second Empire in the Egyptian Revival style at 57 Hancock Street, one of the few in the United States. The Old Suffolk County Court House is another example of Second Empire style. Look for Beaux Arts and Classical Revival details on buildings throughout the walk, reflecting the influence of the École des Beaux Arts in Paris on the American architects who studied there.

❧ THE WALK ❧

The **Old Suffolk County Court House** (recently ①
renamed the John Adams Courthouse) was built in the massive French Second Empire style in 1896, designed by architect George A. Clough. Behind **One Center Plaza in Pemberton Square**, it is on the site of Pemberton Hill, originally eighty feet above the level of the present square, and one of the three original hills the 1630 Puritan settlers named Trimountain. (The three hills were Pemberton, Beacon, and Mt. Vernon; only Beacon remains, in greatly reduced form.) The building's weightiness seems to overwhelm its current

site, diminished in the 1960s when the Government Center was created.

A building with many French associations is the **Boston Athenaeum** at **10½ Beacon Street**, a private or proprietary library built in 1847–1849 and now a New England institution attracting readers, scholars, and researchers from throughout the world. Among the items of French interest is a bust of General Lafayette executed by the famous French sculptor **Jean Antoine Houdon**, noted on the library's guided tour. The Athenaeum also owns the private library of Boston's eighteenth-century French cleric Jean Lefebvre de Cheverus, introduced in Walk Three. In addition, several books in French cover a wide range of subjects. Map lovers will enjoy a large framed edition of a 1755 map by John Mitchell of British and French dominions in North America with French nomenclature. The original was used in the peace negotiations resulting in the Treaty of Paris, 1763. Original copies of the the *Courier de Boston*, the French newspaper published in Boston in the late eighteenth century, the de Cheverus papers, and the French map can be consulted by appointment; telephone 617-227-0270, which also gives the times for guided tours.

The air here is uniquely redolent of both academic indulgence and New England thrift, as welcoming to today's readers as it was to the young Ralph Waldo Emerson who passed many hours here with his carefully assembled reading list. Oriental rugs and a thoughtfully chosen art collection provide a splendid backdrop for the library's extensive collection of more than 600,000 books. Many important historical collections are to be found in the Athenaeum, including the majority of George Washington's library and the personal papers of Henry Knox. The top floor is a scholar's haven, with its vaulted ceiling, long tables for members pursuing individual projects, and alcoves at each window with more tables for study. The building is wheelchair accessible.

Directly across to the right from the Athenaeum is **XV Beacon**, a former office building recently converted to a boutique hotel by Paul Roiff of Heath Properties. The 1903 building was designed by William Preston Gibbons, a graduate of the École des Beaux Arts in Paris. His French training is evident in many details, such as the copper crown molding at the top of the building, small stone balconies, and carvings.

③

To the left of the Hotel XV Beacon you will find a mysterious alley which once led to a graceful brick chapel called the **French Chapel** or *Notre Dame des Victoires*. The private way or alley is called **Freeman Place** and is now occupied by a parking lot.

④

The history of the "French Chapel" began with an innovative Unitarian minister, James Freeman Clarke, step-grandson of the minister of King's Chapel, who built a Unitarian chapel at the end of Freeman Place, the Church of the Disciples, in 1848.

However, when the church's parishioners moved to the more fashionable Back Bay, Freeman's church moved there too, leaving the first building vacant, a common practice in those times. The empty church was eyed by a Father Bouland, a Catholic priest trained in France and ordained in Rhode Island. He had recently won permission from John Joseph Williams, the first archbishop of Boston, to start a church for the city's French-speaking people, who longed to have a place to worship in their native language: descendants of the French military and their families and supporters who stayed here after the Revolution, French Canadians, and Swiss and Belgians who spoke French.

Father Bouland and his flock located their parish church in the former Unitarian chapel and inaugurated it on the second Sunday of Advent, December 5, 1880, naming it *Notre Dame des Victoires*, or Our Lady of Victories. (On that same day two hundred and fifty-one years ago, the cornerstone of *Notre Dame des Victoires* church in Paris was laid, with King Louis XIII in attendance.) Services at the new chapel were said in French, this custom continuing as long as parishioners met there.

"The French Catholic Church in Boston— Boston's first French Catholic Church—is progressing wonderfully. Mass is celebrated daily in the Chapel of Notre Dame des Victoires at the West End. The good pastor, Abbé Bouland, issued a little monthly paper in the interests of his charges. . . ." reports the archdiocesan paper, *The Pilot*, a month later. Word spread in the greater Boston area of the chapel's "outstanding speaker" and soon large numbers of Protestants from Beacon Hill and Back Bay helped fill the chapel's pews to overflowing. Women outnumbered men as a result of another of Father Bouland's gifts, that of charisma; attendance at the chapel became the social thing to do.

Church records state that Father Bouland's projects extended far beyond the modest chapel, however. His vision reached to a sumptuous church on

Columbus Avenue, a charitable bureau, a dispensary, a school, and even a French Université de Boston. To underwrite these costly projects, Father Bouland left for Europe in March of 1881 with letters of introduction from Archbishop Williams in his pocket. We learn much about the young priest when we read that Father Bouland had instructed Archbishop Williams to mention his honorary title in these letters of introduction "for, in Europe," he said, "oftentimes on these depends the success of a cause." He also confided in Archbishop Williams that it was his deepest wish to build a Notre Dame des Victoires in Boston like the one in Paris.

Father Bouland's trip was indeed a success, whether or not a result of his honorary title. Pope Leo XIII at the Vatican greeted him warmly and awarded him the rank of papal chamberlain with the title of monsignor. Monsignor Bouland, the first to use such a title in Boston, returned triumphantly to Boston in 1882 with $60,000 in funds and donations.

But events in the small chapel took a sudden unfortunate turn in the following months. Funds diminished, the whereabouts of the $60,000 were unknown, and the chapel was forced to close for non-payment of rent. Monsignor Bouland returned to Europe to raise more money. Archbishop Williams asked the French Society of Mary, or the Marists, to take over the parish and a wealthy parishioner, Miss Deletang, rescued the church financially.

In spite of these setbacks, the church prospered and grew under the leadership of the Society of Mary until it was necessary to move the parish to a larger building on Isabella Street, this church becoming known throughout Boston as the "French Church." There masses were said in French for the benefit of the French families in the area until recently.

The story of Monsignor Bouland's visions for Boston ends with the interesting coincidence that a city insurance map of 1902 shows a Boston University building at the end of Freeman Place where the French Chapel once stood—a bit of his dream of a Université de Boston made manifest, perhaps.

At the corner of Beacon and Bowdoin Street you will find another site with French overtones, **21–25 Beacon Street**. Imagine a high hill reached by a long flight of stone steps. On top of the hill is a stately stone mansion three stories high with four rooms on each floor. Behind

James Bowdoin II

this imposing building stretch orchards of apple, pear, and quince trees, followed by flowers for display and cutting and vegetables stretching to Ashburton Place, as the street is now known. This was the home of **James and Elizabeth Bowdoin II,** important yet almost unknown participants in Boston's French connections.

James Bowdoin II, third-generation Huguenot, was introduced in Walk Two, reading the Declaration of Independence from the balcony at the Old State House in 1776. He graduated from Boston Latin and Harvard College and was governor of Massachusetts for two terms, from 1785 to 1787. As a son of the "Enlightenment," the eighteenth-century movement promoting reason and humanistic reform, he was a founder of the American Academy of Arts and Sciences, conducted scientific experiments, and possessed a library of one hundred and twenty books, an impressive collection for the times and the mark of a learned man. He was a good friend of Benjamin Franklin, and he and his wife had the honor of entertaining George Washington in their home on Washington's first trip to Boston as president of the United States.

As admirable as these distinctions may be, there is one even more exceptional that does not meet the eye: the achievement of a complete assimilation into Boston's eighteenth-century elite culture. Bowdoin is even labeled in one Boston history book as a "Boston Brahmin." This is a feat of great magnitude as well as a tragic one; the act of assimilation often requires the denial of the original culture, a daring sacrifice in the case of the rich and creative Huguenot heritage. There is no known official mention of Bowdoin's Huguenot heritage at any point during his lifetime or even in the eulogy at his death.

Bowdoin's grandfather, Pierre Baudouin, left France earlier than most Huguenots and thus managed to liquidate his estate in order to take his money with him. He and his family stayed in Ireland for a few years, then sailed in his own ship, the *John of Dublin*, to Maine, where he owned land. Persistent Indian attacks forced them to come down to Boston where they joined the Faneuils and other Huguenot friends. It was James I, Pierre's son, who quickly changed the family's name from Baudouin to Bowdoin after his father's death. James became a successful merchant in Boston shipping and real estate. When he died, his fortune was declared to be the largest in Boston's history.

After he graduated from Harvard, James Bowdoin II entered into political life in the capital, another means of assimilation. He married the obligatory wealthy wife of English descent and high social standing, the sister of his Harvard friend John Erving, Jr. He bought his father-in-law's mansion on upper Beacon

Street (though as difficult as it is to imagine now, it was an area considered unfashionably rural at that time). When Bowdoin's daughter was to be married, orders for wedding finery were sent to England, not France.

As you walk through the Bowdoin home in your imagination, you will see three public reception rooms on the first floor, well furnished with English Wilton carpets and an abundance of silver, including a large tureen (now at Boston's Museum of Fine Arts). In those days, silver was regarded as an accessible bank account.

The bedroom on the second floor was furnished with red damask curtains, pillows, bedspread, and hangings. A room on the third floor used for scientific experiments contained five telescopes, a microscope, an air pump, and an orrery, a mechanical model of the solar system.

Bowdoin also owned several horses and carriages. The horses were let to graze on the Common on land owned by the artist John Singleton Copley. As was the custom among wealthy Huguenots and those of Huguenot descent, he owned many slaves.

Bowdoin's rise as a statesman began with his post as one of the four Boston representatives in the provincial legislature of Massachusetts, then as a member of the Council advising the governor. Illness kept him from attending the first Continental Congress in Philadelphia; John Hancock went in his place. Then followed his two successful terms as governor of Massachusetts. When the Massachusetts Convention met in 1788, both Bowdoin and his son, James III, were delegates. Statesman and scholar, Bowdoin brought both leadership and culture to Boston, and served it well. Bowdoin's son James III established Bowdoin College in Maine with gifts of land, money, and his extensive art collection.

⚓

But this is not the end of the history of th[...]
1843 Bowdoin's large mansion was razed, [...]
other two mansions in the same block. The e[...]
were broken up into small lots, which were soon occupied by brick bowfront houses. The property containing Bowdoin's house was called the Mansion Estates. One of these brick bowfronts, **17 Beacon Street,** was bought in 1858 by Dr. Dio Lewis, a rotund gymnast from Concord. Lewis turned the building into a seven-story private temperance hotel. Turkish baths were added in the basement; Lewis claimed the baths gave quick relief from "catarrh, rheumatism, torpid liver, and general dulness."

A young girl who was with a family staying there gave the new hotel the French name **The Bellevue**—the beautiful view. Author Louisa May Alcott was a frequent guest and spent many winters writing in her "sky parlor" near the building's mansard roof.

The French associations here continue. Dr. Lewis's hotel was torn down in 1899 and replaced by the elegant brick and limestone

Mascarons on the Hotel Bellevue

Hotel Bellevue, designed by architects Peabody and Stearns in the Beaux Arts and Classical Revival styles. Peabody's training at the École des Beaux Arts in Paris influenced his use of ornate balconies, elaborate stone carvings, and iron lamps. In 1925 an addition on the left side of the Peabody and Stearns Building by architects Putnam and Cox extended the French theme; Cox also had studied at the École des Beaux Arts. Architectural details here typical of the Beaux Arts style include the Parisian mascarons, or carved faces, on the building's lower façade, and bull's-eye windows.

It was at this newly rebuilt hotel that aviator Charles Lindbergh stopped during a tour after his triumphant 1927 crossing of the Atlantic from New York to Paris, the first first solo transatlantic flight. He traveled in a motorcade up Beacon Street and, surrounded by crowds of fans, was swept into the Bellevue Hotel for a welcoming celebration. His famous winning smile and casual bareheaded style made him popular on reserved Beacon Hill.

The Bellevue's days as a hotel ended in 1983 when the building was converted to condominiums. This corner of upper Beacon Street, however, still preserves the memories of Bowdoin's presence, as well as existing examples of the French Beaux Arts style.

On Beacon Hill, in an area now partially occupied by the east wing of the Massachusetts State House, once lived patriot and Boston Tea Party member, **William Molineaux**. For centuries many Boston histories have listed him as an Irishman. But it seems possible that because of his obviously French name he could be a Huguenot who fled to Ireland, as did the Baudouins. When he left Ireland and arrived in Boston, the literal-minded customs officials could have assumed that his country of origin equaled his nationality; or Molineaux, fearing reprisal from France, could have given his nationality as Irish.

Nor has assimilation stopped even in the present, as the story of Walter Lucier proves. Walter grew up in Boston in the 1970s in a predominantly Irish neighborhood, went to school with the boys in the area, played sports with them, and assumed that he was Irish. In junior high school, on his first day of French class, his teacher looked at his attendance list and commented on Walter's classic French name. The boy protested, "Oh, no, sir, I'm Irish." But when Walter questioned his parents at dinner that night, they said, "Yes, we're French, but we thought letting you think you're Irish would make it easier for you." (See the section "So You Think You're Irish.")

The **Amory-Ticknor House** at **9 Park Street** was built for the wealthy merchant Thomas Amory in 1803–04 by Charles Bulfinch, and was the largest house in Boston at that time. In the walls of the cellars were floor-to-ceiling brick caves suitable for storing the wines Amory was to obtain as a wine importer. Sadly, Amory's ships sank one by one during the building of the house and he was forced to declare bankruptcy just before his housewarming. The high cost of the building made it impossible to sell, so it became an elegant boarding house. Mayor Josiah Quincy secured the building for General Lafayette's use while he was in Boston for the laying of the cornerstone of the Bunker Hill Monument in 1825. Lafayette gave a gala party here for the "ladies of Boston," a topic of Boston conversation for months before and months afterwards.

No introduction is needed for the commanding golden-domed **Massachusetts State House**, designed by architect Charles Bulfinch in 1795–97. After the American Revolution, state leaders wanted a larger and more important state house to reflect the new republic's more prosperous image. The cornerstone was laid July 4, 1795, by Governor Samuel Adams and Paul Revere. Although Bulfinch's architectural influence is largely English, his time with Thomas Jefferson in France studying such buildings as the Maison Carrée, a preserved Roman temple, must surely have been an important adjunct to his architectural education.

Inside the State House are several reminders of Boston's French heritage. Free guided tours are given on weekdays; you can also tour on your own. (The wheelchair-accessible entrance is on the right side of the building on Bowdoin Street.)

Take the elevator to the second floor to locate the following items of interest. At the second floor go to the left to find **Doric Hall**, with its ten Doric columns, practical iron and plaster copies of the original pine columns. As you face the windows, the wall to the right holds a brass plaque, installed in 1992, commemorating Massachusetts LaFayette Day and honoring the outstanding contribution of the General Marquis de La Fayette to the American Revolutionary War, his support of the United States of America, and his contribution to French-American friendship. Massachusetts LaFayette Day was proclaimed in 1935, to be observed on May 20 of each year. (In some places on the plaque the American democratic spelling of Lafayette is changed to the French and more aristocratic spelling of de La Fayette.)

In the next room, dedicated to Civil War nurses, the wall to the left shows a mural of second-generation Huguenot Paul Revere riding to Lexington and Concord to warn the colonists that "the British are coming!"

On the first landing of the stairway rising behind the Civil War nurse sculpture is a bronze plaque in memory of **Lt. Norman Prince**, founder of the Lafayette Escadrille, an American squadron in the French Flying Corps during World War I. The 1916 plaque describes Prince as a "pioneer in the World War French Army 1914 who gave his life in humanity's cause."

Continue walking up the stairs until you reach the third floor. Directly to your right you will see the entrance to the **Senate Chambers**, which is in the original Bulfinch part of the State House. Walk through the anteroom and to the right into the round chamber itself. To your left you will find a marble bust of the General Lafayette, the only foreigner so honored in the room. The General visited the chamber on his way to lay the cornerstone for the Bunker Hill Monument in 1825. The bust presents a very democratic view of Lafayette; no wig, no lace-ruffled collar, only a simple Roman drape.

Down the hallway a large mural depicts the Massachusetts 104th Infantry Regiment being decorated in April of 1918 in Apremont, France—the first military unit in American history to receive this honor from a foreign government. General Passaga, a French officer in a light blue uniform, said, "I am proud to decorate the flag of a regiment which has shown such fortitude and courage."

On November 27, 1945, at Camp Pittsburgh in Rheims, France, the colors of the 104th U.S. Infantry Regiment were again decorated by the Republic of France, for service in World War II. This mural is embellished on the right margin by a depiction of Marianne, a young woman in a red bonnet who symbolizes the French Republic. Kneeling beside her is a young girl with a gold halo, Joan of Arc. A white flag with gold fleurs-de-lis forms the background. On the left margin, a splendid woman, the Statue of Liberty, is posed in front of a white flag with gold stars bordered by red trim. An eagle is at the top of this section of the panel. Battles for the 26th Infantry Division in World War I are listed on the left side and for World War II on the right side.

The State House saw many disruptions even in peacetime. As can be imagined, the State House was the meeting place for many kinds of groups and discussions, not all of them quiet ones. One of them held in 1881 concerned a group of irate French Canadians.

In that year's annual report, **Colonel Carroll D. Wright**, chief of the Massachusetts Bureau of Labor Statistics, described French Canadians as the "Chinese of the Eastern States," adding that they "care not for our institutions, civil, political or educational." He later went on to say that they are a "horde of Industrial invaders, not a stream of stable settlers." After the pros and cons of the truth of these accusations were bandied about in the press, a delegation of sixty French-Canadian leaders presented their case at the State House on October 25, 1881.

The sixty leaders, representing several French-Canadian communities in Massachusetts, cited their accomplishments: since 1850 they had founded some forty church parishes, several service organizations, and many newspapers. They were a peaceful people with strong family ties and a church-centered life. They also spoke about the exploitation of French Canadians by their employers, who often underpaid French workers.

The result of the visit was that Colonel Wright conceded a few points, and promised that the next report would show more balance. In fact, the 1882 report retracted all these harsh and demoralizing accusations as unfair.

Opposite the State House is the **Robert Gould Shaw**
Memorial, by designers McKim, Mead & White, which
is well sited between two elm trees. The sculpture is in
memory of the first regiment of emancipated African-
Americans formed in Boston during the Civil War. They
were led by Robert Gould Shaw, young son of an old
Boston family. Shaw and many of his men died during
the assault on Fort Wagner in South Carolina in 1863.
Sculpted by Augustus Saint-Gaudens, the son of a French
artisan and an Irish mother, the bas-relief memorial took
thirteen years to form in the artist's studio. Saint-Gaudens
also studied at the École des Beaux Arts in Paris.

A tablet in a granite column in the fence in front of
the State House marks the location of **John Hancock's**
mansion and information about its unfortunate
demolition in the late 1800s. The first signer of the
Declaration of Independence lived here during the
American Revolution and while he was governor of
Massachusetts. During the Revolution, the Hancocks
frequently invited officers from the French fleet guard-
ing the port of Boston to lunch at their mansion high
on Beacon Street. "We are covered with attentions at
Boston," wrote Admiral d'Estaing, commander of the
French fleet, in a letter to George Washington.

At one of these luncheons, many more French officers than usual showed up. There wouldn't be enough
milk for the punch! Mrs. Hancock sent all the cooks
and maids to the Boston Common where they made a
flurry of ruffles and lace while they milked cows, any
cows, even the neighbors' cows, to save the day.

⑩ **The Swan Houses** at **13, 15, and 17 Chestnut Street**, on the north side, are an intriguing remainder of a most exotic bit of French lore. Designed by Charles Bulfinch and built around 1804-1805, these three sedate brick houses were gifts from the remarkable Boston heiress **Hepzibah Swan** to her three daughters upon their marriages in 1806, 1807, and 1815. With the houses were three stables around the corner at 50–60 Mount Vernon Street, described later.

Hepzibah Swan, however, lived in a luxurious mansion also designed by Bulfinch in Dorchester overlooking Dudley Street. One of its rooms was thirty-two feet in diameter with a twenty-five-foot-high domed ceiling. Here she and her eccentric husband, Colonel James Swan, amassed a superlative collection of French furniture and fine art objects; some pieces were also placed in the Swan houses on Chestnut Street for the use of their three daughters.

But who was this Colonel Swan? Born in Scotland, he took part in the Boston Tea Party, wrote a book on the United States slave trade, and was a close friend of bookseller and Revolutionary War hero Henry Knox. Swan was wounded in the Battle of Bunker Hill and received the rank of colonel during the American Revolution. After the Revolution he made a fortune in the mercantile business, then became interested in real estate, which took him to Paris in 1787. There he became involved in redressing the United States war debt to the French. He did not want to be paid in hard currency because of the fluctuating market. Instead, his remuneration was in the form of valuable French art and furniture, some from the French aristocracy anxious to dispose of it during the tumultuous years of the French Revolution, other pieces from the new French government emptying its palaces in exchange for funds. In return, Swan, acting as the American agent for the

French government, supplied badly needed American wheat, rice, tobacco, and naval equipment.

At some point a misunderstanding arose during Swan's business dealings, either with a German firm or with a sale of land in Virginia to French nobility (sources differ on this point). To maintain his honor Swan insisted on going to the Paris debtor's prison, Sainte Pélagie. Despite the pleas of Swan's wife and General Lafayette, he spent the next twenty-two years there. He was released in 1830 and died soon after.

Swan is notable as one of America's first collectors of fine European decorative arts, and a discriminating one. Some of his French treasures, recently restored, are on display at Boston's Museum of Fine Arts. (Details of this collection are in "French Icons Outside the Walks.")

Swan Houses

Before we leave the Swan Houses a slight digression will reveal an interesting method of dating the houses you see on these walks, especially in the older sections of Beacon Hill. At number 15 the windows at the street-level floor are smaller than the ones above, because this area was nearest noise and dirt and thus less attractive. Here were the kitchens, the laundry, and other such activities. The floor above, the *piano nobile*, was more important and formal. The windows are much taller on this level than below or above, and sometimes have balconies, as do the Swan houses. Each ascending floor has progressively smaller windows, the rooms less desirable since stairs must be climbed to them, and so better suited as bedrooms or for use as apartments for less affluent people. The rooms at the top, with the small dormer windows in the mansard roofs, were for servants or students and artists. Each building was a microcosm of society.

But the invention of the elevator in the late 1800s reversed all of this. The top floor became the most desirable, with its open view; the rest of the building was less preferable the closer it was to the street with its noise and limited view.

Former home of Samuel Gridley Howe

A famous quotation from Henry James introduces distinguished **Mount Vernon Street**: "The only respectable street in America." Originally on the site was John Singleton Copley's vast pasture; sold by John Hancock, the property eventually was lined with handsome brick houses and mansions.

⑪   **32 Mount Vernon Street** was home to physician and abolitionist **Samuel Gridley Howe,** who organized the Committee of Vigilance to protect fugitive slaves. African slaves sometimes ended up in the French West Indies on their way to America, thus entering into the Francophone culture.

Numbers **50–60 Mount Vernon Street** are the **Swan stables** designed by Charles Bulfinch in 1804– 1805, now converted to dwellings. They were built by Hepzibah Swan for use by her daughters who lived on Chestnut Street at 13, 15, and 17. Mrs. Swan's practical yet rather eccentric ways are evidenced in a nine-foot ramp for carriages and cattle, also designed by Bulfinch, which goes from the stable yards to Chestnut. The height of the stables was restricted to thirteen feet above the street to preserve the view from Chestnut Street. ⑫

Swan stables

At **5 Pinckney Street**, the **Middleton-Glapion House** marks the boundary between the more tra- ditional South Slope of Beacon Hill and the more Bohemian North Slope. Before central heating, a house on the warmer, sunny southern side was more desir- able than the colder north side, occupied by those with thinner pocketbooks. ⑬

This house was built by **George Middleton**, a black coachman and Revolutionary War soldier, and

Louis Glapion, a mulatto barber from the French West Indies. This two-story clapboard house is one of oldest and least changed houses on Beacon Hill.

The **African Meeting House and Afro-American Museum** on Smith Court off Joy Street contain many exhibits about the African-American population of the North Slope. The meeting house was built by blacks to serve as a church in 1806. **William Lloyd Garrison** was responsible for the founding here of the New England Anti-Slavery Society in 1832. By the end of the nineteenth century, many blacks had moved to the better residences of the South End and Roxbury and left Smith Court. The building was bought in the 1970s by the Afro-American Museum. Its contents present another side of Beacon Hill, one seldom seen until recent years.

57 Hancock Street is a rare example of **French Second Empire** architecture in the Egyptian Revival style, one of the few in the United States. Three five-story bays on the front façade end in a mansard roof capped with an Egyptian pyramid shape. It seems to enjoy its unusual role on the North Slope.

French Second Empire Egyptian Revival house

66 Phillips Street was the home of **Lewis Hayden**, ⑯ once a fugitive slave, then a famous abolitionist along with his wife **Harriet**. Not only did they hold many abolitionist meetings at 66 Phillips Street, but their home also served as a station on the Underground Railroad, a series of houses and other safe places where fugitive slaves could hide on their way to free states or Canada.

Hayden claimed that his home had never been searched, a claim given depth perhaps because he kept two kegs of gunpowder in his cellar and vowed to detonate them if anyone tried to enter the house looking for fugitive slaves. Both Lewis and Harriet worked with Underground Railroad "conductor" Harriet Tubman (c. 1820–1913), who was known as a "Moses" for her people as she sought to move slaves to safety. Harriet Hayden left a scholarship to Harvard Medical School for "needy and worthy colored students."

Hayden's three-story red-brick Federal row house is considered to be the most important existing abolitionist site in Boston. A Heritage Guild plaque outside the house reads:

HOME OF LEWIS HAYDEN 1811-1889

FUGITIVE SLAVE, LEADING ABOLITIONIST

PRINCE HALL MASON, RESCUER OF SHADRACH

MEMBER OF THE GENERAL COURT

MESSENGER TO THE SECRETARY OF STATE

———————

A MEETING HOUSE OF ABOLITIONISTS AND

A STATION ON THE UNDERGROUND RAILROAD

THE HERITAGE GUILD, INC.

Josephine St. Pierre Ruffin, African-American editor ⑰ and publisher of *The Women's Era*, lived at **103 Charles**

Street for twenty years. Her grandfather was from French Martinique. In 1894 she founded the New Era Club for African-American women and organized a conference forming the National Federation of Afro-American Women. The New Era Club met at what was formerly the Charles Street African Methodist Episcopal Church and merged with another group in 1896 to form the National Association of Colored Women. Ruffin served a term as vice president, but although a Massachusetts accrediting group approved the New Era Club, the national federation blocked the club's membership, to avoid offending the Southern members. Her husband, George Ruffin, became the first African-American judge in the North.

This walk ends here. Enjoy charming Charles Street with its red brick sidewalks, gaslight-style lamps, and many enticing boutiques and food shops.

Trimountain—Pemberton, Beacon, and Mt. Vernon—
as it looked in the 1700s before it was whittled down
as fill for marshes, ponds, coves, and the BackBay.

The Berkeley

THE BERKELEY

BACK BAY

Belle of the Ball

---------- ⚜ **SETTING THE STAGE** ⚜ ----------

The connoisseur of French architecture has many
rewards in store on this walk. The filled-in swamp of
the Back Bay was a blank slate for urban design and
building in the latter part of the nineteenth century,
when the architecture of France for houses and public
buildings was the prevailing mode, and the Paris of
Napoleon III was the inspiration for city planning.

In this tour along Commonwealth's broad bou-
levard and nearby avenues and squares you will see
ornate mansions, an elegant hotel, and an assort-
ment of churches, all featuring the work of French or
French-inspired artists, architects, designers, sculp-
tors, and craftsmen. Styles include Art Deco, Art
Nouveau, Baroque Beaux Arts, Second Empire, French
Romanesque, French Academic, and even French
Chateauesque.

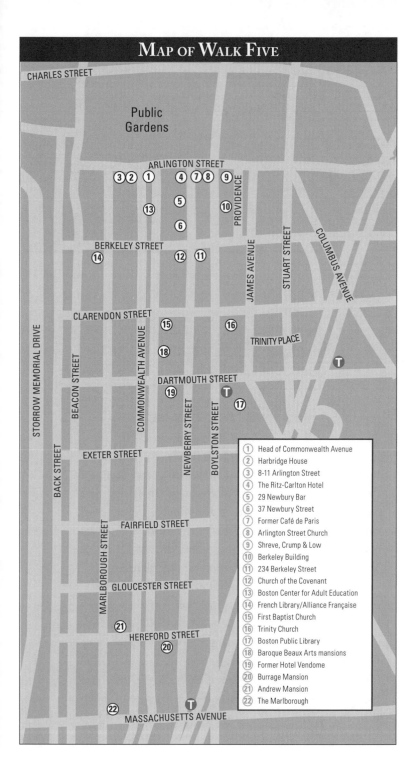

MAP OF WALK FIVE

CHARLES STREET

Public Gardens

ARLINGTON STREET

③② ① ④⑦⑧ ⑨

⑬ ⑤

⑥

BERKELEY STREET

⑭ ⑫ ⑪

PROVIDENCE

JAMES AVENUE

STUART STREET

COLUMBUS AVENUE

CLARENDON STREET

⑮ ⑯

⑱ TRINITY PLACE

Ⓣ

STORROW MEMORIAL DRIVE

BEACON STREET

COMMONWEALTH AVENUE

DARTMOUTH STREET

⑲ Ⓣ

⑰

BACK STREET

EXETER STREET

NEWBERRY STREET

BOYLSTON STREET

① Head of Commonwealth Avenue
② Harbridge House
③ 8-11 Arlington Street
④ The Ritz-Carlton Hotel
⑤ 29 Newbury Bar
⑥ 37 Newbury Street
⑦ Former Café de Paris
⑧ Arlington Street Church
⑨ Shreve, Crump & Low
⑩ Berkeley Building
⑪ 234 Berkeley Street
⑫ Church of the Covenant
⑬ Boston Center for Adult Education
⑭ French Library/Alliance Française
⑮ First Baptist Church
⑯ Trinity Church
⑰ Boston Public Library
⑱ Baroque Beaux Arts mansions
⑲ Former Hotel Vendome
⑳ Burrage Mansion
㉑ Andrew Mansion
㉒ The Marlborough

MARLBOROUGH STREET

FAIRFIELD STREET

GLOUCESTER STREET

㉑

HEREFORD STREET

⑳

㉒ Ⓣ

MASSACHUSETTS AVENUE

This walk also visits two significant libraries. Plan to spend some time at the French Library and Cultural Center/Alliance Française of Boston and Cambridge. In this elegant mansion you'll find a lending library of 25,000 books, periodicals, videos, cassettes, and movies, as well as a range of activities, including lectures, exhibits, and concerts. Even if you don't speak French, there is much to see and do here.

The Boston Public Library had its origins in the enthusiasm of a French count and the example of a French *bibliothèque*, and its realization in the artistry of its French-trained architects and interior designers. The library is also the home of a statue from France that exemplifies the expression "banned in Boston."

Along the way, find refreshment and excitement on busy shopping streets with a French flair.

❖ THE WALK ❖

The Back Bay neighborhood is one of Boston's historic French legacies. The architecture here bespeaks the city's French heritage more than any other part of Boston. Though this area was not inhabited by any known group of French or Francophone residents, it has always been known for its love of things French. Thus, the focus here is not on historical figures but on the neighborhood's French architecture and urban planning.

Commonwealth Avenue is the spine of the Back ①
Bay. The area known as Back Bay, before its liberation into a building site, was a malodorous tidal marsh used as a city dump, a "brackish expanse of anonymous character," as Henry James put it. Beginning in the late 1850s, the Back Bay marshes were filled, with four hundred and fifty acres of buildable land created by 1882.

Architect **Arthur Gilman**, a visitor to Paris, undertook the plan for the new Back Bay, and chose to imitate Baron Georges-Eugène Haussmann's urban design for the Paris of Napoleon III. Haussmann had replaced the city's narrow, dark streets with broad, well-lit boulevards. This was not only an aesthetic choice, but was also designed to prevent crime, unsanitary conditions, and the barricading of narrow streets during rioting.

How did this French influence reach Boston? An important source was American students of art and architecture, many from Boston, who studied at the École des Beaux Arts in Paris. The journey from Boston to Paris had become easier starting in 1830, when the Cunard shipping line chose Boston as its only North American port for Europe-bound ships. Boston architects and artists who flocked to Paris included H.H. Richardson, William Gibbons Preston, Allen Howard Cox, Robert Swain Peabody, and William Morris Hunt, all of them bringing home French art and architecture for Boston's museums and streets.

Arthur Gilman modeled the two-hundred-foot-wide Commonwealth Avenue on the Champs Élysées in Paris. The avenue's open green space, with statues and trees arranged in the symmetrical French style, stretches from the Public Garden to the Fens.

The Public Garden, on the other side of Arlington Street, is an endless parade of colorful flowers in well-trimmed beds, graceful pale green willow trees, a skating pond in winter, and the famous swan boats, all reminiscent of the bright gathering spots for popular entertainment typical of Napoleon III's Second Empire Paris.

Gilman laid out the streets surrounding Commonwealth Avenue in a logical grid, as opposed to the narrow, winding streets of the English style. The streets were even named in an alphabetical order;

however, the streets have English names. Construction began next to Arlington Street and moved westward in the following years. The service streets Gilman added behind each row of houses add another Gaelic organizational touch.

12 Arlington Street is the site of a large Nova Scotia sandstone French-Italianate mansion known as **Harbridge House** designed in 1859–1860 for **Sarah Choate Sears** by Arthur Gilman. To the original house on Arlington Street Gilman joined One Commonwealth Avenue, creating a house large enough to display her outstanding art collection and create a magnificent music room where pianist Ignace Paderewski and violinist Fritz Kreisler were among the performing artists. Among the works of art is a portrait of Mrs. Sears and her daughter by John Singer Sargent.

Continue north to **8-11 Arlington Street**. The *Atlantic Monthly* offices were once at 8 Arlington Street, in the 1920s. The design of four similar houses here, built as a group, restrains the individualism typical of the single large buildings on the Parisian boulevards. The expansive building lots of the grand Parisian boulevards were not available to Boston architects, so they imitated the Paris buildings by massing groups of houses together; from a slight distance the four houses give the impression of a single gigantic building. However, the street remained the most important factor here, not the house. Mansard roofs over the top-floor arched dormers complete this French Academic reinterpretation of classical elements.

(4) Continue back down Arlington Street in the direction of the subway and you are immediately at **The Ritz-Carlton Hotel** at **15 Arlington Street**. Opened in 1927 and modeled after the Ritz Hotel at the Place Vendôme in Paris, it is a unique Boston institution. Everything is proper, elegant, and in place at the sophisticated Ritz. Its quiet Art Deco touches include decorative fans over the exterior second-story windows. Inside, the lobby on the Arlington Street side retains its 1927 appearance, with bronze detailing over the mirrors by the Arlington Street entrance stairs, original electrolier ceiling lights, and raised plaster ceiling embellishments. In the earliest days of the Ritz most of the hotel's occupants were permanent residents, not transient guests. Of the latter, it is said, only those in the Social Register were permitted.

Exit the hotel on the Arlington side and then turn right onto fashionable **Newbury Street**, with its abundance of cafés (several with outdoor tables), art galleries, and boutiques, many of these establishments with a French or Mediterranean flair.

(5) The many outdoor tables at cafés along Newbury Street was explained at **29 Newbury Bar**: since patrons cannot drink at sidewalk tables without eating, too, there are an increased number of outdoor tables, serving both food and drink. Also, smokers who must abide by the no smoking law inside the restaurant can light up at a sidewalk table.

(6) **37 Newbury Street**, a DKNY boutique, is included here since the building resembles Le Corbusier's Carpenter Center at Harvard University. Although this book is devoted solely to Boston's French landmarks,

Le Corbusier's building in nearby Cambridge at Harvard University is not to be missed, since it is his only building in North America. Here at 37 Newbury Street, the glass-block stairwell which runs the building's height is reminiscent of Le Corbusier's style.

Although the **Café de Paris** formerly at **19**
Arlington Street is now closed, its history is of interest to Francophiles. An authentic French import, the café

was shipped piece by piece from Paris in 1979 by Frenchman Oliver Boney. Complete with French refrigerators, a French "proofer" or bread maker, and original faux wood detail, it was set up by Boney as a business for his son. The next owner, Michael Fulchini, continued the largely French menu to the delight of the café's clientele of students, nearby hotel guests, musicians, actors, and those looking for a reminder of Paris. After the management subsequently changed hands, the café closed.

Café de Paris

At the corner of **Arlington and Boylston streets** is the tall spire of the **Arlington Street Church**, constructed in 1859–1861, the first building to emerge from the Back Bay's muddy quagmire. A Unitarian stronghold, the handsome brownstone church is adorned by a striking collection of **Louis Comfort Tiffany**'s stained-glass windows in the French Art Nouveau style. They constitute one of Boston's best-kept secrets; even neighborhood residents seem doubtful when questioned about them. Furthermore, a respectful rivalry between the Arlington Street Church and the Church of the Covenant, a block down Boylston Street, apparently has yet to determine which church has more Tiffany windows.

Tiffany went to Paris in the 1850s to study painting, but was swept away by the sinuous lines and naturalistic subject manor of Art Nouveau as it showed itself in glass. On his return to the United States he formed his own glass company. His work was exhibited at the Chicago World's Fair and the Paris Exposition in 1900, where his studies had begun. His windows in the Arlington Church show his technique of layering the glass to fill the depths of the Impressionistic colors with light. A sunny day when the church is open is best for viewing the magnificent windows.

The façade of Boston's prestigious jewelers **Shreve, Crump & Low** at **331 Boylston Street** displays excellent Art Deco details, a style originating in Paris in the early 1900s. The grillwork below the windows mixes plant motifs with a geometric zigzag design. Stylized pilasters and capitals with columns are also featured. The silver leaf ceiling inside is most appealing and the collection of jewelry, fine crystal, china, and antiques contains many pieces of French origin.

Shreve, Crump & Low

Continue west down Boylston Street. At **420 Boylston Street** is the flamboyant **Berkeley Building**. This Beaux Arts commercial building with its glass and verdigris walls was designed in 1905 by Codman and Despradelle, the latter an architect from France. Unfortunately, inappropriate treatment of the ground floor has marred the entrance, but the central bay's cornice at the building's top with its bright pennants lifts the spirits.

Across the street is an Au Bon Pain restaurant, one of the French-inspired chain described in Walk Two.

234 Berkeley Street is a beautiful specimen of a French Academic public building, one of the few freestanding structures in the area, persisting amid the changing Back Bay landscape. It was designed for the Massachusetts Institute of Technology as a museum of natural history in 1830 by William Gibbons Preston, a student of the École des Beaux Arts. Its rusticated sandstone

234 Berkeley Street

ground floor features two large two-story pilasters, or shallow columns. The building is now home to **Louis Boston**, a clothing store. Some may be surprised to see MIT on the Boston side of the river.

Cross Newbury Street to the corner of **Newbury and Berkeley** where you will find the **Church of the Covenant**. Inside is a sizable Tiffany favrile glass lantern from the 1893 Chicago World's Fair, wired by none other than Thomas Edison. The interior woodwork of the church is also Tiffany-designed, as well as the impressive collection of stained-glass windows.

On the north side of Commonwealth Avenue you will find **5 Commonwealth Avenue**, the Gamble Mansion, better known as the **Boston Center for Adult Education**. Although named for Sara Gamble, a member of the center's board, it was Walter Baylies, a Harvard graduate and rising cotton merchant, who built this extravagant mansion in 1904 for his growing family and retinue of servants. "He liked to cut a dash," his son Edmund once explained of his father. "He liked things just so."

This building contains a glittering ballroom, a replica of a room in the Petit Trianon at Versailles in France. It is currently used for meetings, weddings, and coming-out parties. The brilliance of the room, surrounded on all sides with mirrors and raised carvings, and crystal chandeliers overhead caused an admirer to exclaim, "At night, it just sparkles!" French detail is also found in Mrs. Baylies's bedroom and dressing room on the second floor, and in the dining room, now part of the BCAE office, with its circular Renoir look-alike painting over the fireplace, commissioned in Paris in 1925. The time of private homes in the Back Bay is diminishing—few are kept in their original state—and very few are open to the public. Make an appointment to tour this unusual home if it isn't open during your walk (617-267-9300).

The handsome mansion at the corner of Marlborough and Berkeley streets is the **French Library and Cultural Center/Alliance Française of Boston and Cambridge** at **53 Marlborough Street.** This important nonprofit organization with the formidable title has as its mission "the active promotion of French language and culture for the enjoyment and enrichment of Greater Boston."

⑭

The French Library and Cultural Center was founded more than fifty years ago by an American organization, France Forever, formed to help liberate France during World War II. A lending library of French books and periodicals was part of the group's activities. After the war, director Belle P. Rand sought to enlarge and incorporate the collection as "The French Library in Boston." The 1867 mansion at 53 Marlborough was donated by Francophile Katherine Lane Weems in 1961 and the library has made its home there ever since. The scope of activities widened and the organization became known as "The French Library and Cultural Center, Inc.," in 1993; in 2000 the center welcomed the Alliance Française of Boston and Cambridge to the organization.

French Library/Alliance Française

FLCC/AFBC holds classes of French instruction for adults, business clients, and children. It also maintains a lending library of 25,000 books, periodicals, videos, cassettes, and CD-ROMs, and a popular children's library. Concerts, culinary demonstrations, wine-tastings, book discussions, art and photography exhibits, French movies, and translation services are also offered. Additional programs focus on other Francophone countries, such as Haiti, Senegal, Morocco, Belgium, and French Canada, giving members and visitors a full panorama of French culture.

The center's gracious interiors reflect the elegance for which France is famous. For example, the salon to the left of the central foyer is modeled after the library of Malmaison, Josephine Bonaparte's home outside of Paris.

A popular yearly event for Bostonians is the center's celebration of Bastille Day, July 14, commemorating the storming of the Bastille prison in Paris in 1789, which liberated its prisoners and demonstrated the power of the people over the monarchy. The center's festivities usually include dinner and a street dance; check for the exact date and location.

The French Library and Cultural Center/Alliance Française of Boston and Cambridge also offers antidotes to New England's persisting prejudices regarding things French. Try a weekend movie in French (usually with subtitles) or just browse in the library to absorb some of that Paris-in-Boston feeling.

As you leave the library pause and look at the unusual roofline, another mansard, or "French roof," as nineteenth-century Boston architects called it. (See the description of Old City Hall in Walk One for more information about this distinctive French architectural element.)

(15) **The First Baptist Church** at **Commonwealth Avenue and Clarendon Street** was the first important

commission, 1870–72, of Boston architect Henry Hobson Richardson, and his first use of the Romanesque style, which is charac-terized by massive stone walls and semicircular arches. The church's most outstanding feature is its tower, similar to an Italian campanile, or bell tower. The tower culminates in a frieze modeled by Frenchman Frédéric Auguste Bartholdi, the sculptor of the Statue of Liberty in New York. The frieze depicts the holy sacraments and includes faces resembling famous Bostonians, such as authors Longfellow, Hawthorne, and Emerson, and politician Charles Sumner. The church is also known by another name, "The Church of

First Baptist Church tower

the Holy Bean Blowers," because of the angels with trumpets at the four corners of the tower that seem to be blowing beans down at passers-by.

Trinity Church at **Copley Square**, a National Historic Landmark, is often listed with the Boston Public Library as two of the most influential public buildings in the United States. In 1872 six firms were invited to par-ticipate in a design competition for the church; Henry Hobson Richardson won the commission. Although Richardson was young and then lived in New York—not to be taken lightly in Boston—several of his Harvard classmates were on the building committee and wielded their influence. Richardson, who had trained at the École des Beaux Arts in Paris, submitted a French Romanesque design with elements from other styles, from early Syrian Christian to American colonial. The site presented a challenge: the church's massive tower had to be reduced

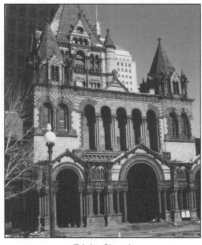

Trinity Church

in weight because it would rest on Back Bay's watery, filled-in land. Even then, to support the tower's ninety million pounds, it had to be placed on two thousand wooden piles arranged in a ninety-foot square.

For the interior, Richardson chose to plaster and paint the interior granite walls, considering the granite too cold to the eye otherwise. Painted walls of gold, blue-green, and sienna emerged. John La Farge and young Augustus Saint-Gaudens produced several works of art for the church, including frescoes, sculpture, and stained glass, both of them of French parentage and, like Richardson, trained in art in Paris.

A direct French influence figures in the completion of Trinity. Richardson did not like the portico's two front towers and asked that they be redone. He sketched a design for a new portico based on St. Trophime in Arles, France, which he visited in 1882; the new portico and two towers were finally constructed more than a decade later.

While Richardson was a student at the École des Beaux Arts in Paris, the American Civil War began, and he was unable to receive funds from his family. He was forced to work part-time as a draftsman while he continued his studies, delaying his return to Boston. This apparent setback turned out to be an asset, since his familiarity with French architecture was greatly increased by his extended stay and work as a draftsman.

The Boston Public Library at **Copley Square** has ⑰ French connections in many directions, beginning with an energetic French count. In the spring of 1841, **Count Nicholas Marie Alexandre Vattemare** arrived in Boston. Vattemare, a French writer, actor, aristocrat, ventriloquist, and philanthropist, had stumbled on a brilliant system of international cultural exchange. For five head-turning years, Vattemare, or Alexandre as he was called in the theater world, had performed with his touring troupe of actors for the titled, rich, and royal leaders of Europe. In these travels he made it a habit to visit local museums and libraries to get ideas for his plays. There he found several duplicate books, medals, and art objects, which he felt could form the base for a free exchange of these duplicates. After receiving no interest from the French government in his plan,

Boston Public Library

Vattemare took Lafayette's advice and sailed for New York in 1839, where he was hailed as the "modern Alexander the Great." He longed to spread the idea of free libraries in the United States, and visited each of the twenty-six states, hoping to leave a trail of librar-

ies behind him, much like Johnny Appleseed's apple trees. However, Vattemare had a setback as he toured the states when he found that most of the so-called public institutions were actually private, which would preclude the opportunity for free exchange.

New England showed signs of recognizing the concept of a library as a public service, so Vattemare turned his attention to Boston. He met with Mayor Josiah Quincy and the directors of several libraries, all controlled by private associations, which Vattemare wished to mold into one institution. The response to Vattemare's enthusiastic ideas

Statue of *Science* outside the library

for a free tax-supported public library in Boston? Tepid. The enterprise lagged. When he returned to Paris, he sent a crate of fifty books in French to Boston as a gift from the city of Paris. These books, the nucleus of the present five million books in Boston Public Library, languished on the third floor of City Hall, then on School Street. Many of the volumes were of a highly practical nature, such as the *Reports of the Labors of the Paris Board of Health from 1829 to 1839* or *Regulations Concerning the Sale of Spirituous Drinks in 1837* (in Paris, that is).

The books stayed in the right top floor room of City Hall for years to come. Eventually, Vattemare's persistent correspondence to Quincy and a second trip to Boston accompanied by more books began to produce action. By April of 1848, with the backing of Quincy, by then a close friend of Vattemare, a statute was enacted to establish and maintain a free public library in Boston for the use of the people of the city: America's first free public library supported by taxation.

Boston's foot-dragging in establishing the library and the city's almost total disregard for Vattemare after the library was built have some interesting roots. Perhaps still-Puritan Boston found Vattemare guilty of being Catholic and French and also of leading an artistic, exotic, theatrical life. Some questioned his personal morals; Harvard professor (and a Boston Public Library founder) George Ticknor and others called him a charlatan. But none could doubt the vigor, idealism, and personal magnetism of the man of whom Josiah Quincy said, "the idea of establishing a free library in this city seemed to pervade him to his fingers' ends."

Statue of *Art* outside the library

A few years later, after much persuasion from Vattemare and despite Boston elitism, Mayor Quincy organized a committee to build the library. Of the firm chosen to design the building, McKim, Mead & White, principal architect Charles Follen McKim had the distinction of attending the École des Beaux Arts in Paris. There he became familiar with the Bibliothèque Saint Geneviève, a library built in 1842–50 by French architect Henri Labrouste. McKim modeled the Boston Public Library after the Bibliothèque: the likeness is remarkable, including the first-floor arched windows and the names of notable figures in the sciences and arts in a frieze above the windows.

Vattemare has been almost completely forgotten—only his name on a tablet in the McKim lobby floor, along with other early supporters of the library, testifies to his brilliance and extraordinary vision. His motto "Give with joy, receive with gratitude" still resounds with integrity over the entrance of the McKim wing.

Lion statue at the Boston Public Library

Inside the library are many outstanding French contributions. Murals by the French artist **Pierre Puvis de Chavannes** decorate the corridor and entire upper portion of the main stair hall in the library's older wing. A man of advancing years, he did not come to Boston to see the site, yet created a work of great harmony. His "The Muses of Inspiration Hail the Spirit, the Harbinger of Light," depicts nine delicate muses from Greek mythology hailing a male figure, the Genius of Enlightenment, against a background of a pale grove of olive and laurel. The steps of the majestic main staircase are French Echaillon marble mottled with fossil shells. At the turn of the stairs are giant twin lions crouched on pedestals, the work of **Louis St. Gaudens**, brother of Augustus, who also sculpted the head of Minerva, goddess of wisdom, on the central keystone over the entrance of the McKim wing.

Yet another French link at the library is an extensive collection of books about Joan of Arc amassed and donated by Cardinal John J. Wright and housed in the Cheverus Room, which features a portrait of **Jean Lefebvre de**

Cheverus, Boston's first Catholic bishop, described in Walk Three. (Recent renovations to this room have made the collection's future location uncertain.)

The two large statues in front of the McKim Building, representing Art and Science, were sculpted by Boston artist Bela Pratt (1867–1917). Pratt studied with Augustus Saint-Gaudens and at the École des Beaux Arts in Paris; his two statues were set in place in 1912.

A statue made in Paris and intended for the Boston Public Library became famous, or infamous, for the uproar it inspired when the library refused it in 1896. "Banned in Boston" began in this era. American **Frederick William MacMonnies** created the bronze *Bacchante and Infant Faun*, a female nude holding an infant aloft with a bunch of grapes in her other hand, as a gift to Charles McKim, in repayment for fifty dollars the architect had given to the young artist when MacMonnies left Boston at nineteen to study art in Paris.

Bacchante and Infant Faun

Boston's initial response to the statue to be mounted in the library's courtyard was favorable, but soon a huge outcry arose. The *Boston Globe* suggested a "nice moral statue instead—perhaps of a Sunday School teacher." A local minister called it "a memorial to the worst type of harlotry." Also against the statue were General Francis Walker, president of the Massachusetts Institute of Technology, and Charles Eliot Norton of Harvard University. Dismayed, McKim withdrew his gift and offered it to the Metropolitan Museum of Art in New York, which was very pleased to receive it.

When the statue was first cast in Paris, the French government ordered a second casting as well. From this, several years later, philanthropist George R. White of Boston commissioned a statue made for the Boston Museum of Fine Arts, where it is now exhibited. For the Boston Public Library's 100th anniversary celebration in 1995, an additional casting from the MFA *Bacchante* was made; finally, after ninety-seven years, she would be brought home to the library, though at first she had to endure obscurity in a dark niche at the top of the grand staircase. The *Bacchante* is now displayed in the center of the library's open courtyard pool, a symbol, perhaps, of MacMonnies's years at the École des Beaux Arts in Paris, of a delayed Boston-Paris reconciliation, and of an acceptance of French culture over old Puritan standards. A detail of the statue appears on the cover of *Boston's French Secrets.*

Two houses at **128–139 Commonwealth Avenue** are rare examples of elaborate **Baroque Beaux Arts** architecture in Boston. The fussiness of the style did not make it a Boston favorite; such gaudiness was left to New York. The balcony at 130 and the fine wrought iron are distinctive. Masses of climbing pink roses in the small gardens and on the façades of the buildings make spring and summer an ideal time to see these houses.

The *grande dame* of Boston hotels, **Hotel Vendome** at **160 Commonwealth Avenue**, has a glorious past. The older corner building was designed in 1871 by prominent Boston architect William G. Preston, who trained at the École des Beaux Arts. One of Boston's outstanding Second Empire buildings, the original cost was one million dollars, then a subject of much debate.

From the beginning, the Hotel Vendome commanded much attention in the Boston press. Built in an elegant French Renaissance style with a façade of white Italian and Tuckahoe marble, it featured bays, balustrades, pediments, and a mansard roof. Condominiums have now replaced the hotel rooms and very little of the original interior ornament remains.

Luxury abounded in the Vendome. Each room had private bathrooms, steam heat, and fireplaces—all innovative for Boston hotels. By 1882 it was Boston's first public building to have electric lights. The Vendome's guest list included French actress Sarah Bernhardt, Oscar Wilde, Mark Twain, General Ulysses S. Grant, P.T. Barnum, and President Grover Cleveland.

The Vendome witnessed a dramatic evening on November 3, 1881, that epitomized the spirit of this French-inspired building. Here an elite group of Frenchmen and their wives were entertained with a reception, dinner, and a ball. They were the direct descendants of the French naval and army heroes of the decisive American Revolutionary battle of Yorktown in 1781, and had been invited to the United States to celebrate its centennial. American and French dignitaries mingled with descendants of the French army's Rochambeau and those of naval leaders de Grasse and d'Aboville, among others. Full military dress heightened by gleaming medals and classic French evening gowns vied with the Vendome's elegant decor and aromatic tropical flowering plants. The *Boston Herald* reported that the Vendome "seemed more like a chateau than a hotel."

No walk down Commonwealth Avenue would be complete without a visit to Boston's real French chateau, the **Burrage Mansion** at **314 Commonwealth Avenue** at the corner of **Hereford Street.** It was designed in 1889 by Charles Brigham, who undertook at the same time the long rear addition to the Massachusetts State House. The mansion is an exception to the city's "no flamboyance, please, we're Bostonians," the French Chateauesque style being something of a rarity here. Prompted by the Château de Chenonceaux in France's Loire Valley, the mansion seduces the viewer with turrets, gargoyles, ornate carvings, decorated chimneys, elegant mahogany interior detail, and a greenhouse with a curved glass roof. Now luxury condominiums, it remains the only Back Bay mansion comparable to New York's Vanderbilt mansion in its size and degree of ornamentation.

Burrage Mansion

The **John F. Andrew Mansion** at **32 Hereford Street** was designed by McKim, Mead & White in 1884–88. Of interest here is the wrought-iron exterior balcony on the third floor just above the Palladian window, rescued from the burning Tuileries Palace in Paris during the Commune revolt of 1871. The house is now occupied by an MIT fraternity, which proudly maintains this artifact from Paris history.

On the south side of **Marlborough Street** at **416** is the very tall apartment hotel **The Marlborough** by architect Willard T. Sears. The term "apartment hotel" was an adaptation from the original "French flat," a concept most likely introduced first in Boston from France, based on the city's high urban density. The first French flats in Boston were at the Pelham Hotel at the corner of Boylston and Tremont streets; see the section in Walk One about the hotel for more information about these choice residences.

The French influence extends deeply throughout these orderly blocks between Arlington Street and Hereford Street. Boston's hidden heritage should be even more apparent after this tour. As you walk through the city, enjoy your new knowledge of Boston's French secrets.

FRENCH ICONS
OUTSIDE THE WALKS

THE MUSEUM OF FINE ARTS

Directions

Take the Green Line E train outbound from Park Street and get off at the Museum stop on the E train. Cross Huntington Avenue and enter the museum on the left side of the building near the parking lot.

The Museum of Fine Arts at **465 Huntington Avenue** in the Fenway area, is a monumental Classical Revival building designed by Guy Lowell in 1907–1909. Originally located on the top floor of the Boston Athenaeum on Beacon Street, this cultural institution is one of the most important in the United States. Its extensive collection of 500,00 pieces and over fifteen current exhibits each year attracts a million and a half visitors. Its director since 1994, Malcom Rogers, has done much to infuse vitality into the museum's previously conservative atmosphere.

Historically, the museum has strong ties with French artists and their art; many of the works collected here were pivotal in the development of art in the nineteenth and twentieth centuries. American art influenced by these important French leaders is also on exhibit.

A list of outstanding French art from the museum's collections chosen by the Museum of Fine Arts staff for the readers of this book follows.

Painting

> Pierre-Auguste Renoir, *Dance at Bougival*, 1883, Sidney and Esther Rabb Gallery
>
> Claude Monet, *Poppy Field in a Hollow near Giverny*, 1885, Sidney and Esther Rabb Gallery
>
> Paul Gauguin, *Where Do We Come From? What Are We? Where Are We Going?*, 1897, Sidney and Esther Rabb Gallery
>
> Jean Baptiste Greuze, *Young Woman in a White Hat*, about 1780, Ann and William Elfers Gallery
>
> François Boucher, *Halt at the Spring*, 1765, Ann and William Elfers Gallery

Decorative arts

> Swan set of eighteenth-century French furniture, Ann and William Elfers Gallery
>
> Pair of sauceboats with stands, François-Thomas Germain, 1756–59, Charles C. Cunningham Gallery
>
> Pair of ice-cream coolers, from the Service aux Liliacées, Sèvres, 1802–05, Leona R. Beal Gallery
>
> Edgar Degas, *Little Fourteen-Year-Old Dancer*, statue, original model, 1878–81, cast after 1921, Sidney and Esther Rabb Gallery
>
> François Auguste René Rodin, *Psyche*, statue, 1898–99, Sidney and Esther Rabb Gallery

In October of 2003, the museum opened a newly installed gallery, the Ann and William Elfers Gallery, on the second floor of the Evans Wing, for an important set of eighteenth-century French royal furniture from its Swan collection. Comprised of ten pieces of gilded wood furniture by the renowned Jean-Baptiste-Claude Sené, it is the only complete set of eighteenth-century French royal furniture in the United States. Recently, the set has undergone a complete restoration made possible through the efforts of the MFA staff of curators and conservators as well as colleagues in Los Angeles and Paris. The installation relates how the set survived the past centuries and was restored to its original splendor. It also documents in detail the long process of restoring and reuniting these outstanding pieces.

Pieces from the Swan collection

The Swan collection was amassed by Bostonian Colonel James Swan while he was the American agent for the French government during the French Revolutionary period. The pieces were donated to the MFA in the twentieth century by Swan's descendants. The set of gilded furniture made for Marc-Antoine Thierry de Ville d'Avray, the administrator of the royal furnishing stores, was intended for his bedchamber and consisted of a bed, two armchairs, four side chairs, a *bergère* (chair with upholstered arms), a *prie-Dieu* (kneeling chair), and a fire screen.

Other pieces from MFA collections add to the elegance of the gallery: paintings by François Boucher,

Jean-Baptiste Greuze, and Elisabeth Vigée-Lebrun; and eight outstanding painted and gilded wood *boiseries* panels from the estate of another Boston collector, Peter Parker. Portraits of James Swan and his wife Hepzibah painted by American artist Gilbert Stuart from the museum's Art of the Americas collection are also featured. (See Walk Four for more about Colonel Swan's interesting history.)

The Museum of Fine Arts and the cultural service of the Consulate of France organize the annual *Boston French Film Festival*, now a leading festival of French films in the United States. The MFA also regularly exhibits work by contemporary French artists.

The museum's café, restaurant, and gift shop can complete your visit here. The museum is wheelchair accessible.

BOSTON SYMPHONY HALL

Directions:

Take the Green Line E train and get off at the Symphony stop; Symphony Hall is in front of you.

Boston Symphony Hall at **301 Massachusetts Avenue** is home to the world-renowned Boston Symphony Orchestra, considered by some the "largest French orchestra" in existence, so great has been the French influence on this august group. Conductor Pierre Monteux set the tone early in the twentieth century, followed by Charles Munch, conductor until 1962. Numerous French soloists have performed over the years.

Although the orchestra has taken on a more international tone in the following years, the French influence persists. Recently, the orchestra played the American debut of a work by the French composer Eric Tanguy.

The cultural services of the French Consulate maintain an active relationship with the Boston Symphony's director.

THE ISABELLA STEWART GARDNER MUSEUM

Directions:

Take the Green Line E train and get off at the Museum stop. Walk down Huntington Avenue; turn right on Louis Prang Street, which runs into Fenway. The museum is at 280 Fenway.

The Isabella Stewart Gardner Museum at **280 Fenway** contains several French pieces of art collected by its extraordinary owner Mrs. John Lowell Gardner, Jr. The exterior of the building is plain, but the interior is a four-story palace built around a central courtyard full of colorful flowers, statues, and fountains, designed to resemble a Venetian palazzo.

When Mrs. Gardner suffered a deep depression after the death of their two-year-old son, her doctor advised her and her husband to take an extended trip to Europe for her health. On her return to Boston she became a controversial member of Boston society. Stories circulated about "Mrs. Jack," as she was called, walking down Tremont Street with a lion on a leash; proper Boston was often shocked by this woman born not in Boston, but in New York.

Isabella Gardner's subsequent trips abroad deepened her interest in art by the great masters of the

Italian Renaissance. She began to collect art seriously with the aid of Bernard Berenson, a young art historian and recent Harvard graduate, including several French pieces. The first Matisse to be shown in a museum in the United States, *The Terrace, St. Tropez*, is here. The seal she designed for the museum, a shield bearing a phoenix, the symbol of immortality, carries the French motto, *C'est mon plaisir* (It is my pleasure).

In her will Mrs. Gardner bequeathed her home as a museum "for the education and enjoyment of the public forever," stipulating that nothing be changed after her death.

This list of ten outstanding pieces of French art in the museum was prepared by the museum's staff.

Henri Matisse, *The Terrace, St. Tropez*, Yellow Room

Edouard Manet, *Madame Auguste Manet*, 1863, Blue Room

François Boucher, *The Car of Venus*, Little Salon

Jean Baptiste Camille Corot, *Noonday*, n.d., Blue Room

Edgar Degas, *Madame Gaujelin*, 1867, Yellow Room

Rosa Bonheur, *A She-Goat*, 1899, Blue Room

Ferdinand Victor Eugène Delacroix, *The Crusader*, n.d., Blue Room

Beauvais or Gobelin tapestry, 1755-1775, *Amorino Offering Flowers to a Sleeping Nymph*, Little Salon

Mid-twelfth-century sculpture *Two Kings*, from Notre-Dame-de-la-Couldre, Parthenay; Spanish Cloister (the other "Two Kings" are in the Louvre)

Gustave Courbet, *A View Across the River*, Blue Room

The museum café provides a pleasant place for lunch, and the nearby gift shop has unusual mementos; both are wheelchair accessible as are most of the galleries.

THE PAUL REVERE HOUSE

Directions

Take the Green Line. Get off at Government Center. Keeping Boston City Hall on your left, walk towards Faneuil Hall. Go down a flight of stairs. Proceed in the same direction. North Street will be to your left. Continue up North Street. The Revere House is ahead one and a half blocks, and will be on your left.

The Paul Revere House at **19 North Street** was purchased by Paul Revere in 1770. His father, Apollos Rivoire, a Huguenot, left France when he was thirteen to escape persecution; in Boston, he changed his name to Revere. His son Paul neither spoke, wrote, nor read French. It is only within the past several years that his identity as a Huguenot descendant has been confirmed. (More about Revere's Huguenot background is in Walk One.)

Paul Revere House

The Revere House is thought to be the only original colonial dwelling remaining in the center of a large city in the United States. Like many houses of the period, its small frame was made larger by a second-floor overhang, or jetty. It boasted leaded windows for light and visibility. Revere owned this house for thirty years, and it was a departure point for his many missions for the Revolutionary cause, including his famous ride to warn the colonists that the British were coming. The Revere House has preserved some of the furnishings used by Paul

Revere, his wives, and his sixteen children, including silver made in the Revere shop. In addition, the Revere House gives us an ideal view of everyday life in colonial Boston, in surroundings colored by a French sensitivity to fine design. There are forty Revere silver pieces in the Paul Revere House collection and six pieces of furniture, which were used by the Reveres. The museum is handicapped accessible for the first floor only.

Revere located his cannon and bell foundry in 1792 on the lower part of nearby Foster Street where he manufactured church bells, stoves, hollowware, and cannons until the roof blew off in 1804! Soon afterwards, all business was transferred to rural Canton.

Revere was present at the laying of the cornerstone of the Massachusetts State House on July 4, 1795. He also provided 789 pounds of nails and almost four tons of copper for the construction of the State House dome; he was able to roll the copper thinly enough so it could cover a curved surface. (The dome remained copper until 1874 when the current gold-leaf was applied.) This unique artisan, inventor, and patriot was also the first in America to operate a financially viable mill for rolling sheet copper.

You can also explore the brick **Pierce-Hitchborn House** next door at **29 North Square**, the home of a first cousin of Paul Revere. When you are ready to return follow the red bricks of the sidewalk forming the Freedom Trail to the Haymarket stop on the Green Line.

These sites outside the main walks add to our discovery of the many French facets of Boston, past and present —and no longer secret!

So You Think You're Irish

My name is Sean Fitzgerald and you tell me my heritage is French? There must be a mistake here. No, the strange circumstances of Irish-French interactions over the centuries have produced many Frenchmen and women who think they're Irish. There is a strong bond between England and France based in some part on their common Celtic heritage and their geographic proximity.

How is the origin of a name forgotten or obscured? People can lose their heritage for several reasons: exile because of persecution, famine, or economic difficulties; a deliberate name change for protection or advancement; invasion, war, defeat, and slavery can also take away homeland and name.

Ireland has been the fertile soil for a great interchange between the two cultures as a result of the Norman-French invasion of England in 1066, and the arrival of French Protestants in the late 1600s and early 1700s, fleeing persecution.

1066 seems a long way off to make any difference in peoples' names today, but scholars tell us differently. By the time the Norman-French conquered England, they had been using last names for fifty years. In their hereditary system, a person was named according to his dwelling place, occupation, physical traits, or other identifying words. The names were first given to the king, then the higher nobility, the lesser nobility, landed gentlemen, peasants and so on. It took years for this naming to be finished. Meanwhile, those without a last name were obviously of lesser social status than those who had one. Perhaps that is why Europeans have always been shocked by the casual first-name greetings used by Americans. To be just plain John in this system would place you very low in the pecking order.

The Irish, on the other hand, had already been using a surname, or last name, but had another method for bestowing them—the patronymic system. A name beginning with "Mac" denoted "son of," and "O" denoted grandson. Dermott MacNeal would be Dermott, son of Neal; Sean O'Toole was Sean, grandson of Toole. When the Norman-French conquered England, the English were quick to give their sons Norman first names to seek favor with the conquerors, but the Irish held on to their Celtic names.

The English also began to use Norman last names in the hereditary system. Thomas le Clerc, later Leclerc, was a name derived from the man's occupation as a clerk. John le Fort meant John the Strong. The French-Norman names spread throughout England. In Irish regions, however, the Normans, as they intermarried, started using the Irish patronymic system. Instead of adding "Mac" on the first names of the sons, though, they used "fils," the word for son in French, which the Irish and Normans pronounced "fitz." Sean Fitzgerald meant Sean, son of Gerald, in this version of the Irish patronymic system.

This leads to the famous Norman Fitzes. Scholars say that if your name is Fitzgerald, Fitzgibbon, Fitzharris, Fitzhenry, Fitzmaurice, or similar you are definitely of French origin, not Irish—quite a shock for some and for others a reason for rejoicing. Then, as the Normans settled down and intermarried, they became hibernicised and started to drop the Fitz. That means that a name still retaining a Fitz in front can be dated back quite far. In 1465 all Irishmen living in the Pale (the counties of Dublin, Meath, Louth, and Kildare) were ordered by English King Edward IV to swear an oath to take an English name.

The "Fitzes" are not the only Irish names that can claim French origins. In fact, twenty percent of the names in eastern Ireland have French origins, such as Lacey, Purcell, and Powers.

Many French Protestant Huguenots fleeing French Catholic persecution in the sixteenth through the eighteenth centuries came to Ireland. Their names, such as Deveraux or Molineaux, are used in Ireland as Irish names when in fact their origin is French. Boston's William Molineaux is a good example. A Huguenot, he escaped to Ireland after the revocation of the Edict of Nantes in 1685 meant a renewal of persecution by French Catholics. From Ireland he came to Boston, where his nationality was listed as Irish, not French. The customs official could have made a mistake, but it is highly likely that Molineaux changed his nationality from French to Irish for safety. Molineaux took part in the famous Boston Tea Party, was a courageous fighter in the American Revolution, became a successful Boston merchant, and lived near what is now the east wing of the State House in one of the most pretentious houses of its time. For nearly three hundred years since he has been listed by some historians as an Irishman! No wonder we remain ignorant of the great accomplishments and contributions to Boston's history made by many French émigrés.

Help in tracing an Irish name back to its French origins is available from the New England Historic Genealogical Society at 101 Newbury Street in Boston (617-536-5740). You can research material yourself there for a day fee with the help of a library assistant. Or you can call the library and arrange to pay a staff member for research services. The society has specialists in tracing Irish names back to their French origins. Your local library also has information about other genealogy services throughout the country.

Online, use www.newenglandancestors.org or the website of the Church of Jesus Christ of Latter-day Saints, www.familysearch.org. Enjoy your search—you might find some interesting surprises.

Bibliography

Baird, Charles W. *History of the Huguenot Immigration to America*, Vol II. New York: Dodd, Mead and Co., 1885.

Chartier, Armand. *The Franco-Americans of New England: A History.* Translated by Robert J. Lemieux and Claire Quintal; revised and edited by Claire Quintal. Worcester: Institut Français of Assumption College; Manchester: ACA Assurance, 2000.

Forbes, Allan and Paul Cadman. *Boston and Some Noted Émigrés.* Boston: State Street Trust, 1938.

Hammond, Charles Arthur. "'Where the Arts and the Virtues Unite': Country Life near Boston, 1637–1864." PhD diss., Boston University, 1982.

Kershaw, Gordon. *James Bowdoin II.* Lanham: The University Press of America, 1991.

Quintal, Claire. *Sur les Traces de l'Héritage Français en Nouvelle-Angleterre: Boston.* Bedford, New Hampshire: Centre National de Développement de Matériel pour les Langues Française et Portugaise, 1977.

Scudder, H.E., ed. *Recollections of Samuel Breck.* Philadelphia: Porter & Coates, 1877.

Southworth, Susan and Michael. *The Boston Society of Architects' AIA Guide to Boston.* Old Saybrook, Connecticut: Globe Pequot Press, 1992.

Unger, Harlow Giles. *Lafayette.* Hoboken, New Jersey: John Wiley and Sons, Inc., 2002.

Vicero, Ralph D. "Immigration of French Canadians to New England, 1840–1900: A Geographical Analysis." PhD diss., University of Wisconsin, 1968.

Whitehill, Walter Muir. *Boston: A Topographical History.* Cambridge: Belknap Press of Harvard University Press, 1968.

Chronology

1066	The Norman invasion of England, Battle of Hastings
1572	St. Bartholomew's Day Massacre
1598	Edict of Nantes by Henry IV of France
1605	Samuel de Champlain and Sieur de Monts land in Massachusetts Bay, Boston
1630	England claims Boston as a colony
1674–1763	French and Indian wars
1685	Revocation of Edict of Nantes by Louis XIV
1775	American Revolution begins
1776	American Independence declared
1777	Lafayette arrives, commission as major general in American army by Congress
1778	Franco-American treaty signed, first official act of alliance
1783	American Revolution ends
1789	French Revolution begins
1799	French Revolution ends
1799–1804	Consulate under Napoleon Bonaparte
1804–1814	First Empire, with Napoleon I as emperor
1824–1825	Lafayette visits the United States
1852–1870	Second Empire, Reign of Napoleon III, nephew of Napoleon I
1914–1918	World War I
1939–1945	World War II

French Restaurants

This sampling of Boston French restaurants is from a list courtesy of the French Library and Cultural Center/ Alliance Française of Boston and Cambridge. Try them out for lunch or dinner to add to the French flavor of your Boston tour. The restaurants range from formal to informal and the cuisine from Parisian to regional. Calling ahead for reservations or to confirm schedules is advised. Be adventuresome and try an appetizer or entrée you've never had before. And dust off your high school French!

Aquitane
569 Tremont Street
617-424-8577

Aujourd'hui
The Four Seasons Hotel
200 Boylston Street
617-351-2071

Beacon Hill Bistro
Beacon Hill Hotel
25 Charles Street
617-723-1133

Brasserie Jo
The Colonnade Hotel
120 Huntington Avenue
617-425-3240

Café Fleuri
Le Meridien Hotel
250 Franklin Street
617-451-1900

The Federalist
XV Beacon Hotel
15 Beacon Street
617-670-2515

Hammersley's Bistro
553 Tremont Street
617-423-2700

Julien
Le Meridien Hotel
250 Franklin Street
617-956-8752

Mantra
52 Temple Place
617-542-8111

No. 9 Park
9 Park Street
617-742-9991

Sel de la Terre
255 State Street
617-720-1300

Tangierino
83 Main Street, Charlestown
617-242-6009

Index

Sites by Address

About the Author

RHEA HOLLIS ATWOOD

❧

Rhea Hollis Atwood, writer, independent historian, and lecturer, has given walking tours and lectures about Boston's French landmarks for the Boston Center for Adult Education, the French Library and Cultural Center/Alliance Française of Boston and Cambridge, Boston College, and the Bostonian Society.

While a resident of Paris for two years, Atwood studied French culture and language at the New York University Center. In 1998 she presented "The Bowdoins: An Illustrious Boston Huguenot Family" at the Northeast American Society for Eighteenth-Century Studies. She has carried out research at the Musée de la Marine and Centre du Protestantisme Français in Paris and New York's Huguenot Society of America in addition to the Boston Public Library, the Boston Athenaeum, Boston College, and other Boston institutions.

Atwood's interest in French art and culture led her to form an import business specializing in antique French botanical engravings and lithographs; her love of travel has taken her throughout Europe, to Russia, Israel, and India, to eastern and northern Africa, and also to the Caribbean.

Atwood has written feature articles on Beacon Hill's historic sites for the *Beacon Hill Times* and on Boston's French heritage for the French Chamber of Commerce newsletter. She is also the author of *Upper Beacon Hill* (Arcadia Publishing, 2002).

Atwood was a resident of Boston for ten years prior to moving to California in 2002.

About the Photographer

RAFAEL MILLÁN

Rafael Millán, originally from southern Spain and currently of Watertown, Massachusetts, has been living and taking photos in the United States for more than forty years. Many of his photos have appeared in books, and he has had numerous exhibits since his first U.S. job as a photographer, taking pictures of children with Santa Claus in a Philadelphia department store. He has also written, edited, designed, printed, and overseen the production of many books.

Publishers of his photographs include Macmillan, Grolier, Greystone Press, Blaisdell, Addison Wesley, Heinle, D.C. Heath, Jones and Bartlett, and Newbury House. His photographs have been exhibited in Philadelphia, Cordoba, Cambridge, Sudbury, and Watertown.

Rhea Atwood recounts facts about the 300 year-old relationship between Boston and France. With intelligence and passion she tracks down the French stories and French history. She must have French blood in her veins.

—DANIEL JOUVE, Paris resident and author of *Paris: Birthplace of the U.S.A.: A Walking Guide For The American Patriot*

I highly recommend Boston's French Secrets for its insights into the history of the French in Boston.

—COMTE GILBERT DE PUSY LA FAYETTE

Rhea Atwood's sound knowledge of the history of Boston and of France, her relentless detective work and her engaging style make *Boston's French Secrets* an essential guide—as entertaining as it is educational.

—JEFF FLAGG, Department of Romance Languages and Literatures, Boston College

The way to uncover secrets is to take a close look. This book looks at Boston with a sleuth's eye and reveals its hidden French history and architecture in its storied walks.

—SONIA LANDES, co-author with Alison Landes of *Pariswalks*

This book is a must-read for anyone interested in Boston's French "connection." The author has ferreted out little-known but fascinating facts about the city's many-layered ties to France, its culture, and some outstanding French personalities who played prominent roles in the city's history and development as well as in the crucial early years of this nation. These "walks" will enhance any visit to Boston—for long-time residents of the city quite as much as for out-of-towners.

—CLAIRE QUINTAL, Founding director emerita, Institut français, Assumption College, Worcester, Mass. and Chevalier de la Légion d'honneur, Author of *Sur les traces de l'héritage français en Nouvelle-Angleterre: Boston*

Through a walking history of events imprinted on the streets and buildings of the city, *Boston's French Secrets* exceptionally displays the continuous French presence in and contribution to Boston. A guidebook de rigueur for every francophile!

—M.THIERRY VANKERK-HOVEN, Consul General of France in Boston